1978

WORLD ON A STRING
The Story of Kites

Books by Jane Yolen

WORLD ON A STRING

GREYLING

THE EMPEROR
AND THE KITE

THE MINSTREL
AND THE MOUNTAIN

Jane Yolen

WORLD ON A STRING

The Story of Kites

THE WORLD PUBLISHING COMPANY

CLEVELAND AND NEW YORK

Published by
The World Publishing Company
2231 West 110th Street
Cleveland, Ohio 44102
Published simultaneously
in Canada by
Nelson,
Foster & Scott Ltd.
Library of Congress catalog
card number: 68–26976

Designed by
Jack Jaget

For
my father,
Will Yolen,
with love

Table of
Contents

Acknowledgments

My largest debt of gratitude goes to my father, Will Yolen, who turned over his kite files to me, files which cover over twenty years of clippings, notes, and books.

Special thanks go to Clive Hart of Australia who, in the midst of working on his authoritative book on kites for an adult audience, managed to send me his complete bibliography and to answer innumerable questions.

Thanks, too, to Robert Ingraham, president of the American Kitefliers Association, and F. Rankin Weisgerber, the "Dean of Kite Fliers," for their help; to Mrs. Elizabeth Blakslee of the Field Memorial Library; to Surendra Bahadur of the Go Fly A Kite Store; to Bob Gonter, a kitenik with an editor's eye. And a long-overdue word of gratitude also to Francis "Rog" Rogallo who, some twenty years ago, introduced kites into the lives of the Yolen family—an introduction that radically changed our quiet mode of living.

And finally, my special thanks to my mother Isabelle Yolen who baby-sat on innumerable occasions so that I could finish my research; and to my husband, David W. Stemple, who lived through this book with me.

9

Prologue

A kite is a contract of glory
That must be made with the sun . . .

—LEONARD COHEN

This is a world in which doing rates higher than dreaming. And
we are a generation that has forgotten the twice-told tales our
fathers and their fathers knew. Most adults live in a world bounded
by the tick-tocks of the clock, remembering only that once upon
a time there were such things as dreams.

But there are a few mystics left, men who sow bright papers
into the wind and reap a contract of glory, men who can still link
the visions of childhood with the ticking of those relentless clocks.
Kite fliers are such men.

Kite flying is not really a laughable occupation, though kite
fliers have been ridiculed, railed at, ruled against—indeed, even
persecuted—throughout their two-thousand-year history. Most people distrust the loner, the man who will not run with the pack.
And the kite flier is both of these: mystic and solitary.

He is a mystic because, with his simple kitestring as an umbilical
cord, he nourishes himself from the sky, from infinity. The kite

becomes a means of projecting the man into something greater than himself. It is both symbol and tool, the means and the ends of communion.

The kite flier is also a loner because kiting is, above all, a sport which challenges the single sportsman, thrown back on his own resources, challenged by the wind and sky. It is true that kite flying can be a team sport. The Japanese have a twenty-man team that annually hoists a kite which weighs close to six hundred pounds. And many men and women have been flown on kites that were lofted by teams of loyal companions. But kite flying is first, and essentially, an individual activity.

A man, a string, a kite, and the vastness that is the sky. In many ways the kite flier is cousin to the fisherman, the hunter, the trapper. No matter how many enthusiasts take up the ancient sport, he will always remain a little apart. He is alone and looking upward, experiencing a quiet, personal joy.

Yet, while each kite flier remains a solitary dreamer, he is also part of a working dream. Kiting is one of those singular activities whose history is as exacting as the actual act. Bridges, airplanes, aerial cameras, wireless radio—our knowledge of these and many other devices is at least partly due to the magic of those colorful toys that have led man to explore the air and the air waves. It seems almost as though man has pulled himself up by his kitestrings.

Yes, the man who stands anchor to a kite not only stands in the long stream of history which reaches far back into folklore of the East and up beyond the launching pads at Cape Kennedy, but he is also a living link between the beauty of earth and sky. He sails with his kite on the dipping windwheels of the night. He soars on its wings into the birdsongs of the day.

JANE YOLEN
Conway, Mass.
February 1968

WORLD
ON A
STRING
The Story
of Kites

The East—
Where
Kiting
Began

Kite flying is an ancient sport. It goes back at least two thousand years. Some say it even goes back to the days when men first wondered about the wind and sky.

The kite's ancestors are the leaves that spiraled to the ground and the birds that rode the currents of air before the eyes of primitive man.

No one person could have organized kite flying, laying down rules, or making it into a rigid sport. Instead, kiting sprang up in China when the world's civilizations, like the sun, were rising in the East.

No one can say for certain exactly where in China kites began, or exactly when, or who was responsible for their beginnings. The scholars have their guesses. One scholar suggests that the kite derives from the bull-roarer, an ancient

Kite flying in China was celebrated in the work of early artists, as in this detail from a scroll by Su Han-ch'ên, the renowned twelfth-century painter.

religious object, made of wood tied to a thong, that lets out a noise when whirled. Another feels that the first kite was a Chinese farmer's reed hat held on by a string. A third thinks the kite is related to the old method of shooting an arrow with a string attached so that neither arrow nor prey is lost. And a fourth feels that the kite began as the personal flag or banner carried—and then flown—by Eastern nobility. And so the guessing continues. But however they disagree on the how and when and why, the scholars do agree on the where; in China, several thousand years ago, the first kites were flown. From there, kites spread to Malaya, to Polynesia, to Japan, to Egypt, and finally westward across the great ocean to Europe and the New World.

As the kites spread throughout the Eastern world, the

early civilizations started boasting of their kites in special stories. These stories were handed down from father to son, inscribed on men's minds long before men learned to write on stone, papyrus, or paper.

One of the oldest of these stories comes from the Malayan peninsula. There, about two thousand years ago, the natives worshiped a god of the wind, a god who pushed the palm fronds back and forth and washed the waves upon the shore.

To please the wind god, the Malayans built kites of leaves stretched on bamboo frames. With twisted ropes of vines, they flew their kites as offerings to the wind god. And for many years they were undisturbed on the beaches.

But then, in the sixteenth century, Portuguese explorers came to their shores and the rites were in danger of being profaned. So, the once-open beach flights became secret and mysterious. From their ships, the foreign sailors often saw green kites fluttering over the islands. Yet, when they landed, the sailors would find nothing but occasional bamboo frames floating in the channel waters. It was not until the years brought traders, explorers, and finally scholars to the mainland that the secret of the sacred kite flights was revealed at last.

About a thousand years later, another island people used kites in their religious rites. The Polynesian islanders worshiped twin gods, Rongo and Tane. These brother gods were kite fliers and Tane was pictured as a kite himself, a kite that was constantly catching his long tail in a tree.

It is said that Tane challenged Rongo to a kite contest to see whose kite would fly higher. Rongo, who was the elder twin, secretly provided himself with an enormously long string and so he won. Because of this, when the Polynesians flew their kites, the first up in the sky was always named for Rongo and was dedicated to him. In later years, these kites were often five feet in length. Covered with native cloth, they had long tails ornamented with bunches of feathers and yellow *ti* leaves.

Though the island peoples have the oldest oral tradition about kites, the earliest written kite tale occurs in Egypt. For many years scholars had tried to decipher the hieroglyphics on a particular Egyptian stone. The stone pictured men with their arms upraised. From their arms, lines ran up to the top of the stone. At first glance, the lines seemed to be cracks or scratches. Closer study showed them to be part of the relief. Yet none of the scholars could seriously believe that the lines were meant to be kitestrings, as one professor humorously suggested.

But kitestrings they were!

Later, a papyrus scroll found in the ruins of Elephantine in Egypt, a papyrus dated five hundred years before Christ, helped the archaeologists to decipher the stone and to reveal the entire tale.

It seems that there was a Pharaoh who wanted to rid himself of a particularly clever vizier named Ahikar. In order to discredit him, the Pharaoh summoned Ahikar from Assyria and ordered the vizier to build a palace midway between heaven and earth. If Ahikar failed to build such a palace, he would be put to death.

However, Ahikar's wit was as quick as his reputation was brilliant. First he ordered two young eagles to be captured. He trained them to fly while he controlled them with lines attached to their legs. Soon Ahikar could make the birds dip and soar at his command. Next he trained the eagles to carry two small boys upon their backs. When both boys and eagles were ready, Ahikar brought them before the Pharaoh.

The boys mounted the birds and they sailed upward, nearly one hundred feet above the ground. They looked as though they were, indeed, halfway between heaven and earth.

Then, as Ahikar had instructed, the boys cried out that they were ready to begin building the palace. But they needed brick and mortar. They begged the mighty Pharaoh to fly up to them with the necessary materials.

The Pharaoh was supposed to be a god. And as all gods can fly, so the Pharaoh was thought to be able to fly. But he knew—and Ahikar knew also—that he could not fly. Yet the Pharaoh could not admit this in front of his court. It would be the same as admitting that he was an impostor, that he was not the real Pharaoh. So the Pharaoh was forced to concede that he had just been testing Ahikar for he knew that the sun god would not want his view of earth obstructed. The palace, therefore, was not built, but the vizier had saved his own life and enhanced his reputation. And the story was recorded first on stone, then on papyrus.

Since it is doubtful that a vizier, no matter how brilliant, could have trained eagles to fly with young boys on their backs, many scholars believe that the proper translation is "kite" and not "eagle." (Other scholars, believing that the kite did not reach the Near East until as late as the sixth century, discredit the entire story.) In some languages, the words kite and bird are remarkably close since the early kites almost always resembled birds. In English, for example, a kite is also a kind of hawk. In Maori, too, *kahu* means both kite and hawk. The Greek word *áetós* is kite and eagle. The Chinese say *feng-cheng*, kite and wind-bird. And though boys riding on the wings of eagles is an impossibility, there have been many kite riders in the two-thousand-year-long history of kites.

The earliest written record of kite flying that is accepted by most scholars comes from the second century B.C. in China where the philosopher Liu Ngan wrote that the great Mo-Ti, a fourth century genius, "made a wooden kite which took three years to complete. It could indeed fly but after one day's trial, it was wrecked. His disciples said, 'What

In Oriental countries, kites such as these Chinese figure kites were brought to a high degree of design.

skill the Master has to be able to make a wooden kite fly!' But he answered, 'It is not as clever as making a wooden ox-yoke peg. They only use a short piece of wood, eight-tenths of a foot in length, costing less than a day's labor, yet it can pull 30 tan [nearly two tons], travel far, taking great strain, and lasting many years. Yet I have worked three years to make this kite which has been ruined after one day's use.' Hin-Tzu heard of it and said, 'Mo-Ti is indeed ingenious, but perhaps he knows more about making yoke pegs than about making kites.' "

Also from China comes the tale of an early kite rider.

This type of early kite-balloon, the Dragon Balloon, was flown for the amusement of adults rather than of children.

According to one interpretation of the *Annals of the Bamboo Books*, the Emperor Shun escaped from a tower where his enemies had imprisoned him when his daughter flew a kite made of two umbrella-shaped reed hats up to his window. The Emperor grasped the lines and floated to safety. Yet another version of the tale says that Shun's wicked parents tried to have him killed. His father ordered him to build a granary and when the boy was inside, his parents set the building on fire. Shun spread out two reed hats and jumped from the top of the granary. The hats billowed out, and he parachuted to safety.

21

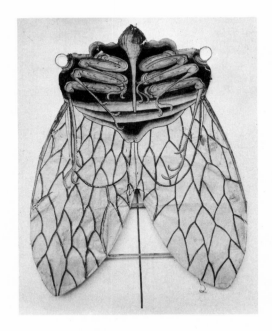

A Chinese figure kite—this one, in the shape of an almost too realistic fly

The Greeks, not to be outdone, have credited the philosopher Archytas of Tarentum (400–365 B.C.) with the invention of the kite. A friend of Plato's and a contemporary of Mo-Ti's, the distinguished Archytas was an outstanding military commander, geometrician, civic leader, and natural scientist, as well as a fine flute player. Besides the kite, Archytas is said to have invented the screw, the pulley, and, as a generous gesture to the children of his slaves, the rattle. However, it is now generally believed that he did not invent a kite at all but a flying machine that was much more complex—and in the long run, less successful. It was a wooden pigeon that was balanced by a weight suspended from a pulley and set in motion by compressed air escaping from a valve—a sort of precursor of the jet airplane.

Malaya, China, Egypt, Greece—these countries claim the

oldest kite stories in existence. And some scholars add that the kite may have even originated as a symbol for the soul of man. They say that the Oriental seamen, when they saw the sail of a boat suddenly blow off in a high wind, connected this with the life—and death—of man. And so the kite was born, a sail or soul held fast by a thin thread.

Perhaps it was so, for in the East there is still much mysticism and mystery attached to kites. In fact, a ninth-century Buddhist monk once wrote:

> *My kite rises to celestial regions,*
> *My soul enters the abode of bliss.*

But whatever the true "oldest" story of the kite may be, it is a fact that kites were brought to a high degree of design and performance in the East long before they were introduced into the West. It was not until the sixteenth century that explorers returning from the Far East brought kites in large numbers to Europe and, later, to the Americas.

Today the Eastern countries still use kites in many religious and national celebrations, and the making of kites is considered a sophisticated art. In the West, too, kiting flourished—but in a different and characteristic way. In the East the kite became mystical and mysterious. In the West, the kite became useful.

The West—
Where Kites
Expanded
Horizons

When the European explorers returned from their trips to the East, they brought home silks and spices, jewels and gold, and tales of rare birds and rarer beasts. This much is common knowledge. But the explorers also brought home a new-found toy, though this is not often mentioned in the history books. They brought home the kite. The Dutch sailors in particular returned with gay-colored Chinese kites for their children.

In the West, the kite was at first an exotic toy. In the beginning kites were used at fireworks displays and were considered somewhat magical. In fact, the first description of the kite in English occurs in a book by John Bate published in 1654 and entitled *Mysteries of Nature and Art*. Bate wrote:

Western explorers brought back kites from their Oriental trips, and the young European boys took up the sport with enthusiasm, as shown in this nineteenth-century line cut.

You must take a piece of Linnen Cloth of a yard or more in length; it must bee cut after the forme of a pane of Glasse; fasten two light stickes crosse the same, to make it stand at breadth; then smeare it over with Linseed Oyle, and liquid Varnish tempered together. . . . then tie a small Rope of length sufficient to rayse it unto what heighth you shall desire. . . .

And even before Bate's book, kites were mentioned in a book on natural magic by the Italian Giovanni della Porta in 1589, and in a German manuscript of 1405. The first printed use of the word "kite" in English appeared in J. Babington's book *Pyrotechnia* in 1635.

But typically, the western scientist soon claimed the kite as his own, using it to open many doors to the universe. Benjamin Franklin's kite was not the only one carrying a key. While there is much evidence that the Eastern kite had been used at times for navigation and weather forecasting by the seagoing Polynesians and for sporadic military ventures by the Chinese and Japanese, scientific kite flying in the West not only flourished but for a long time obscured the plain joy of the sport.

Around the turn of this century, many weather observations were being made with kites. In 1890, the chief of America's weather bureau at Washington, Professor Willis L. Moore, announced that "upper air exploration may be accomplished by a train of kites carrying automatic instruments." Professor Moore's listeners may have been amused

John Bate's book The Mysteries of Nature and Art, *which was the first book in English that described a kite, also carried this woodcut.*

or astounded by his statement, but the truth is that Moore was more than one hundred years behind the times.

Many of the greatest eighteenth century mathematicians—Sir Isaac Newton, Jean Le Rond d'Alembert, Leonhard Euler—had devoted some of their attention to kites. And as early as 1749, two University of Glasgow students made the first recorded weather experiments with kites. Alexander Wilson and Thomas Melville wanted to discover if the air above the ground was colder or warmer than the air on the ground. It was still thirty years before the first balloon flight and about 150 years before the first airplane, so it was only natural that the Scottish scientists used the only controllable flying machine they had—the kite. They made six paper kites and tied a small thermometer to each. Each thermometer, in turn, was tied up in a bundle of paper strips. This was to keep the delicate instruments from breaking when they fell to the ground. Slow-burning fuses were tied to each bundle. Finally, there was a white ribbon attached for visibility. When the fuse burned the string that bound the bundle to the kite, the white ribbon, waving and twisting in its downward plunge, would signal the experimenters.

Wilson and Melville were successful and wrote about their experiments, but for some reason the papers lay neglected for over seventy years. It was not until 1825 that Professor Wilson's memoirs were published in England and reprinted, two years later, in America. There they were read by the eminent meteorologist James Espy who had been experimenting with weather kites on his own. Though he had been preceded by a few years by the Reverend George Fisher and Captain Sir William Edward Parry, who took weather readings from a kite flown over the island of Igloolik in 1823, an island off America's northeast coast, it was Espy and later the newly formed Franklin Kite Club that did much of the pioneer weather work that excited interest in Europe and America.

Although Espy and the Franklin Kite Club were dedicated scientists and kite fliers, the club members were not above practical jokes as well. The club met once a week at the Philadelphia City Hospital grounds for "the purpose of making electrical experiments." It happened that once, while they were flying a kite, the club members noticed a cartman passing directly under the copper wire which was used as a kitestring. The cartman was watching the kite as it danced in the sky and so the club members told him to reach up and grab the wire to see how hard the kite pulled. The innocent cartman did as directed, though he had to stand up on his cart, one foot on his horse, in order to do so. When he touched the wire, he received a shock which passed through him and his horse as well. The horse jumped, the man turned a complete somersault—and the club members roared with laughter.

The work that Espy and the Franklin Kite Club did was exciting to scientists for a period of ten years, from 1835–1845. But then there was a period of almost forty years when kite flying fell from favor because newly invented weather balloons absorbed the attention of the experimenters. Then, as suddenly as it had been dropped, the kite again came into prominence when, in 1883, Englishman E. Douglas Archibald attached an anemometer, a windmeter, to his kites to measure the wind's velocity some 1200 feet above the earth.

From then until nearly the middle of the twentieth century, kite flying for meteorological purposes was pursued with a vigor and dedication that almost rivals the building of rockets of today. Many people and places were involved, but some, of course, stood out above the rest.

For example, on February 4, 1891, William A. Eddy used five kites to lift a self-recording Hicks U thermometer. This was the first automatic record of the temperature in the air. Though Eddy's kites were among the first at Boston's famed Blue Hill Observatory, he is not remembered today primarily

A meteorologist launches a box or Hargrave kite, a favorite of weather watchers up through the early twentieth century.

as a weather scientist but as an inventor. He is credited with the invention of the Eddy kite, a tailless kite with a bowed crosspiece. It looks a great deal like an archer's bow with a loose covering. It is somewhat ironic, though, that Eddy should be noted for the *invention* of tailless kites. After all, the Javanese had been using them for centuries!

Meteorologists in Arlington, Virginia, watch as a Hargrave kite carries a meteorograph aloft in weather tests in the early 1900s.

In 1895, Blue Hill Observatory had gone from the tailless Eddy to a newer kite, the box or Hargrave kite. It was named after its inventor, an Australian named Lawrence Hargrave. And the box kite, because of its greater lifting surface, remained thereafter the favorite of the weather men.

In 1895, also, Professor Charles F. Marvin—who later became Chief of the U. S. Weather Bureau, a position he held for twenty-one years—began using kites for weather observations. And in the early 1900s, box kites were sent up regularly by the U. S. Weather Bureau, taking the place of the manned weather balloons. These box kites were made of spruce wood covered with cloth rather than paper, for the cloth was much sturdier. The scientists would send up the kites four, five, or six at a time in a "train" or "tandem." The reason for this, as explained by a U. S. Department of Agriculture Bulletin of the period, was that a single kite would not make a dependable high trip because the wind is not uniform nor does it increase uniformly with altitude. By distributing the kites along the line, "the maximum lifting power of a given surface can be realized, without at any time exposing the whole of this surface to sudden changes in the pressure of the wind." In other words, it was steadier and more reliable to use a number of kites than just a single one.

With so many kites in the air, record flights could certainly be made. And so they were. November 29, 1905, in Lindenberg, Germany, the Prussian Aeronautical Observatory sent up a train of six kites to a height of nearly four miles. In 1910, on a beautiful May day, the meteorologists at Mount Weather in Virginia sent up a train of ten kites and set the world's high-flying kite record—23,835 feet. That means the kites were about four and a half miles in the air. And they used eight and a half miles of piano wire as guidelines in order to keep the kites from breaking loose. For years that record has stood, though recently there have been kite scholars who claim that, on August 1, 1919, the Germans put up a kite 31,955 feet over Lindenberg.

By this time—the beginning of the twentieth century—many European and American meteorological services were using kites regularly. They obtained information about temperature, humidity, and velocity of the air. In America the ordinary Hargrave kite was used. In Russia, instead of the rectangular-sectioned box kite, the scientists created one with a semicircular section and a curved part to face the wind. In England, the section was diamond-shaped since it was simpler to construct. And in most cases, the kites had thirty to eighty square feet of sail area. There were kite stations in India in 1905, in Egypt in 1907, and in Jutland in 1902–1903 as well as the large posts in Europe and America.

The first permanent government-established station for kite flying in Europe was at Viborg, at the extreme north of Denmark. The governments of Denmark, Sweden, and France cooperated in building and manning it. At the station was a tower some thirty-three feet high mounted on circular rails that could be rotated. It was left open on one side so that whichever way the wind blew, the gap was turned in that direction. An operator sat inside and from his position was able to watch the kites and work the windlass to which the strings—made of steel wire—were attached.

From 1898 until 1906, the U. S. Weather Bureau had seventeen kite stations, mostly in the Mississippi Valley. In

Weather work with kites is still carried on occasionally in the universities. Here Colorado State University weathermen loft a variation of Jalbert's "kytoon."

1907, a regularly scheduled program of kite observations began. The number of stations fluctuated up and down yearly until 1933 when the last single station was operated by the government. Nowadays only an occasional weather station—such as the one at Colorado State University—uses kites to send instruments into the clouds.

Today, with dirigibles and gliders, airplanes, helicopters, weather rockets, balloons, and satellites, we tend to forget that organized, scientific weather-watching began with the kite. The kite flights may now be outmoded, unwieldly, and to some people even seem silly. But just the same, for a long time the kite was all that the weather men had, and it served them faithfully and well.

While weather experimenters are the forgotten heroes of kite flying, the best known scientific flier in history is undoubtedly Benjamin Franklin. There is much irony in this, for Franklin flew his famous kite only as a substitute measure. And he was certainly not *discovering* electricity, though many people mistakenly believe that is what he did at the time of the flight.

The fact is, electricity was already known in the eighteenth century. Experimenters before Franklin had worked with it, using the Leyden jar, the first electrical condenser. And while no one knew precisely what else to do with this newly captured electricity, it became a popular carnival display. Traveling electricians went about Europe exhibiting the phenomenon and selling shocks. One of these travelers, a Dr. Spence, found his way to Boston in 1746 and there Benjamin Franklin had his first look at electricity.

But Franklin did not have the kind of mind that said, "Isn't that fun," and stopped there. He felt that electricity could and should be *useful,* and his experiments with it changed it from a mere curiosity to a source of power.

Other investigators had suggested that the feeble electricity stored in the Leyden jar had something in common with lightning, but no one was certain how to prove this. It was Benjamin Franklin who first suggested that "the top of some high tower or steeple" be used to hold a rod of iron to attract the natural lightning. But Philadelphia, where Franklin lived, had no place high enough. While Franklin was puzzling this out, his suggestion was seized upon by three Frenchmen—Buffon, Dalibard, and De Lor. They found a high point in France and actually proved Franklin's theory for him. But before he learned of the French success, Franklin had decided to fly a kite and use it instead of a high tower. He would fly it and prove that lightning electricity and the mysterious but feeble electricity he could produce in his laboratory were one and the same.

This is why, in June of 1752, one stormy day, Benjamin Franklin and his twenty-one-year-old son William went out to fly a kite. Franklin wrote:

Make a small Cross of two light Strips of Cedar, the Arms so long as to reach to the four Corners of a large thin Silk Handkerchief when extended; tie the Corners of the Handkerchief to the Extremities of the Cross, so you have the Body of a Kite; which being properly accommodated with a Tail, Loop and String, will rise in the Air, like those made of Paper; but this being of Silk is fitter to bear the Wet and Wind of a Thunder Gust without tearing. To the Top of the upright Stick of the Cross is to be fixed a very sharp pointed Wire, rising a Foot or more above the Wood. To the End of the Twine, next the Hand, is to be tied a silk Ribbon, and where the Twine and Silk join, a Key may be fastened. This Kite is to be raised when a Thunder Gust appears to be coming on, and the Person who holds the String must stand within a Door or Window, or under some Cover, so that the Silk Ribbon may not be wet; and Care must be taken that the Twine does not touch the Frame of the Door or Window. As soon as the Thunder Clouds come over the Kite, the pointed Wire will draw the Electric Fire from them, and the Kite, with all the Twine, will be electrified, and the loose Filaments of the Twine will stand out every Way, and be attracted by an approaching Finger.

34

A period mezzotint of the famous electricity experiment. Luckily Benjamin Franklin followed his own instructions and flew his kite from "under some cover."

And when the Rain has wetted the Kite and Twine, so that it can conduct the Electric Fire freely, you will find it stream out plentifully from the Key on the Approach of your Knuckle. At this Key the Phial may be charg'd; and from Electric Fire thus obtained, Spirits may be kindled, and all the other Electric Experiments be perform'd, which are usually done by the Help of a rubbed Glass Globe or Tube, and thereby the *Sameness* of the Electric Matter with that of Lightning compleatly demonstrated.

How would this experiment prove useful? If, as Franklin reasoned, lightning and man-made electricity were the same, it would be possible to protect buildings with an iron rod on the roof that was connected to the earth with a wire. The current would then rush down the pole to the wire and be conducted to the ground where it would do no harm. And Franklin was right. So the most famous kite flight in history led directly to the invention of the lightning rod—and indirectly to the harnessing of electrical power.

Less scientific than either the weather flights or Benjamin Franklin's experiments but just as useful are the kites that have helped build bridges.

There is a Chinese legend about a general who flew a kite across a river to a waiting foot soldier. With the kitestring, a larger rope was pulled across. Then another. And another. Finally a rope bridge was built and the general's army could cross over.

Perhaps T. G. Hulett, the engineer who built the bridge across the Niagara River in New York, had that story in mind. Or perhaps he thought up the idea by himself. Either way, in 1848, the first bridge to span the river at Niagara Gorge was completed because of a kite.

The Niagara River is swift-flowing. Its bed is rocky. And at the time the bridge was being built, ice floes made crossing by boat impossible, even though the river was only 800 feet across at that point. It looked as though the bridge would have to be postponed until spring at least.

It was then that T. G. Hulett had an idea. He put up posters in the nearby town, offering ten dollars to anyone who could fly a kite across the gorge. Many boys came out to try, but the swift air currents carried the kites down into the river instead of up and over the swirling Niagara.

A full day of kite flying, and not a single kite managed to span the gorge. Finally, all the boys but one, Homan Walsh, went home. Young Homan was determined to win.

He had already lost one kite to the ice floes of the river. But just after dusk had fallen, his second kite made it across to the other side. Three men, who had taken the long winding trail around, caught it. Then Hulett attached a heavy rope to the kitestring and the men on the other side hauled it over. Then a larger rope. And finally a heavy-wire cable was pulled across the gorge.

Because of a young boy's kite, the Niagara suspension bridge was begun.

Weather-watching, electricity, bridges—what next? What other new worlds were discovered on the end of a kitestring? Aerial photography was a fourth.

Though aerial photography began in 1858 when a Frenchman made photos from the gondola of a balloon, the world of aerial pictures was made available to ordinary people by means of the kite. In 1887, the English meteorologist E. D. Archibald fastened a large and bulky camera to a kite by four strong strands and took the world's first photographs from a kite.

The French were next to take up the sport. A. Batut, in 1889, sent his diamond-shaped kite into the sky with a slow-burning fuse to trip the camera's shutter. One of his first pictures was that of a French farmhouse. His equipment, as described in the *Photographic Times* of that period, included a kite "with a long tail, assuring stability when it has ascended into the regions of the clouds. The cord holding it to earth is attached to a frame by a sort of trapeze. . . . The kite employed is about seven and a half feet in height. The camera weighed 1200 grams [almost three pounds]." Batut later wrote a book about his experiences.

It took six years before kite photography reached America. When it did, it was William Eddy who experimented with it first. Four years after he began his weather work, Eddy made his first aerial photographs using the tailless kite he had invented and a Bullet camera. Instead of a fuse to

Late nineteenth-century photographers, following the lead of Archibald in England, took aerial pictures by suspending their cameras from kites. They followed instructions and drawings such as this one from an encyclopedia of the period.

trigger the shutter, Eddy used two strings. One was for the kite itself, the other ran directly to the lever control for the camera's lens shutter. In that way Eddy felt that he had more control over his photographs. He also experimented with eight cameras that he fastened to a round, flat piece of wood. Each camera was pointed in a different direction. When a series of tandem kites pulled the floating platform aloft,

Eddy could take eight pictures simultaneously. When laid side by side, the developed prints showed the complete circle of the horizon.

On May 25, 1895, Gilbert Totten Woglom first experimented with five kites that lifted a basket of homing pigeons. At 900 feet, the pigeons were liberated by means of an extra string attached to the main cord. The experiment was to test the kites' ability to pull a dead weight. Satisfied with the performance, Woglom and a friend—George E. Henshaw, an expert amateur photographer—sent up a camera on September 21, 1895, and took the first kite-line photographs of New York City.

Most early aerial photography was strictly an amateur's game. But by 1898, the U. S. Army became interested in the idea and adopted it for reconnaissance work in the Spanish-American War. The tailless Eddy kite with a camera attached was flown over enemy lines and pictures were taken of the disposition of the troops.

In the early 1900s, a professional photographer in Illinois, George R. Lawrence, built a camera and kites to fly it. He was determined to take the largest photograph ever from a "captive airship," as he called the kite. His camera was heavier than a piano, with a bellows longer than most automobiles, and on the ground it took fifteen men to move it. With this giant, Lawrence was able to get his picture. When it was printed, it was so big, it could completely cover the mattress of a single-size bed. In 1906, Lawrence sent his giant camera up by means of a train of seventeen kites and flew it over San Francisco after the famous earthquake. The result was a historic photograph, and Lawrence sold fifteen thousand dollars' worth of prints. Later, Lawrence traveled through the western states taking photographs from his kite and specializing in pictures of the Grand Canyon.

Each of the scientific kites carried something on its flight.

Tetroons (top), a variation of the Jalbert "kytoon," have been used in the 1960s in air pollution tests.

During World War II, American life rafts (left) contained kites as normal survival equipment. They were used to carry emergency radio antennae aloft.

The weather kites carried instruments to measure wind pressure, velocity, and temperature. Aerial photography kites carried, naturally, cameras. Bridge-building kites carried larger and larger strands of rope. Franklin's kite carried a small piece of wire to attract lightning. And Guglielmo Marconi fastened an antenna to a kite in 1901 when he tried to receive a wireless message sent across the Atlantic.

Marconi, who is credited with the invention of the first wireless in 1896—though others had paved the way—had never sent a message across the ocean. But five years after perfecting his telegraph, the twenty-seven-year-old inventor wondered if transatlantic signals were possible.

He decided to try it, and stationed a friend in Cornwall, England. Meanwhile, Marconi proceeded to Signal Hill at the entrance to the harbor of St. John's in Newfoundland. There he fastened a wire antenna to a kite, a gigantic kite capable of lifting a man (it had actually done this in the Boer War which took place in South Africa in 1899). Another wire led from the antenna to a small receiver which Marconi held in his hand.

On December 12, at a pre-arranged time, Guglielmo Marconi flew his kite. At the same time, his friend in England flashed the letter S in code on the wireless. The signal was picked up by Marconi's kite-flown antenna—weak but intelligible—and carried down the second wire to the receiver. It was possible to send messages many miles away. The world was made smaller because of Marconi's kite.

Marconi's antenna was the first of its kind, but not the last. Admiral Richard Byrd carried kites on his polar expedition for emergency antenna use. During World War II, American life rafts contained kites as part of the normal survival equipment. Attached to a special radio by a wire, the kite could be flown easily by a shipwrecked sailor. The hourglass-shaped radio was held between the sailor's knees. By turning a crank on top of the transmitter, the sailor could broadcast over the wire kite line a constant SOS that could be picked up for miles.

And as late as 1967, the Nuclear Research Associates in the United States were using kites to provide high and stable antennae for low radio frequencies. These kites were of magnesium and nylon.

Radios, cameras, lightning rods, weather stations, bridges —these are some of the things kites have helped to develop in the West. And kites were useful in other ways, too. In 1823, Captain G. C. Dansey of the British Royal Artillery proposed that a rescue kite might be used on stranded vessels, and in 1859, an Irish priest, Father E. J. Cordner, designed such a rescue device. It consisted of multiple hexagon kites for lifting people to land, and it was patented in the following year. Kites relayed telephone messages in the late 1890s. About the same time, a Princeton University archaeological expedition used Eddy kites and a boatswain's chair to explore the top of a hitherto unreachable mesa in Albuquerque, New Mexico. And in 1904, fourteen-year-old Frank Seyfang ushered in the era of aerial advertising when he flew a kite

Man-lifting kites have been mentioned in many of the oldest kite stories and figure in many of the newest tales too. This is a modern man-lifter, the Jalbert parafoil, a kind of kite-balloon-parachute.

at the St. Louis Exposition with an ad for corsets fluttering from the strings.

At one time the U. S. Forest Service used kites to scatter tree seeds in order to study the effects of air currents on their distribution. The University of Washington, needing a silent way to loft an automatic camera to photograph spawning salmon, used a kite-balloon invented by Domina Jalbert. These kite-balloons, called "kytoons," have also been part of recent Antarctic antennae experiments; they have flown like airborne buoys over harpooned whales to mark the kill for Norwegian whalers; they have been used in Colorado State University "cloud-snooping" work; and they have taken part in air-pollution tests in Columbus, Ohio. The Jalbert "kytoon" looks like a balloon, is shaped like an airplane wing, and is inflated by having air blown into it.

The list could go on further, but one of the kite's major uses has not yet even been mentioned. It is at once the most obvious and the most important: air flight. The kite is the grandfather of all air travel—from gliders to airplanes to rockets that take men out of the atmosphere and the vehicles that will finally let them re-enter it. If the ancestors of the kite were indeed the birds that crested the currents of air before the eyes of primitive man, kites have remained true to their beginnings. For in the end, it has been the kite that has helped turn man into bird.

Man
Into
Bird

How long has man wanted to fly? Probably since he watched the first birds soaring freely above the earth. All the early tales of flying gods and goddesses, of winged horses and magic carpets indicate how deep in man's heart lay the desire to fly. Even the psalmists wrote: "O that I had wings like a dove." Many hundreds of lives have been lost through the centuries as men vainly tried to imitate the birds.

To imitate the birds—that was the problem! Men tried building feathered replicas of birds' wings; tried running and flapping their arms; tried jumping off houses and barns and cliffs and mountainsides. And they paid for their foolish attempts with broken limbs if they were lucky, or with their lives if they were not.

The few early aeronauts that were halfway successful

were not these men who imitated the birds. The first successful fliers were those who flew on kites. But it was not until
the inventors could free themselves of both the flapping
birds' wings *and* the kitestrings that men truly left the
ground.

This last jump to freedom happened in the nineteenth
century in the West. And almost all the experimenters with
heavier-than-air machines used or considered kites as important parts of their experiments.

George Pocock, an English kite enthusiast, is an example
of these nineteenth-century inventors. After raising a giant
kite into the air, Pocock attached four strong ropes to the
string and from the ropes suspended an ordinary chair. His
young daughter climbed onto the chair and was lifted above
the ground. Next Pocock used a special chair and rig to raise
his son to the top of a cliff. The four ropes this time were
attached to a metal ring and the ring attached to the kite
line by a clasp. While Pocock and two friends flew the
enormous kite, the boy settled himself into the chair and
was soon flown up to the cliff top. There he got out, stretched
his legs, then settled back in the chair again. Once in the
chair, he opened the restraining clasp and chair and young
Master Pocock floated slowly back down to earth.

But George Pocock, like so many early flight experimenters, was not sure where to go from there. He had the
glimmering of an idea, but he had not the spark of genius
to turn that glimmering into a workable thesis. A man who
had such genius was Sir George Cayley.

It was Cayley who made what is considered the original
version of a modern airplane.

The idea of birds' wings beating at the air had been a
tenacious one. But while others had contented themselves
with studying birds' wings, Cayley was studying kite wings
as well. In 1804, Sir George constructed a successful model
aircraft with kite wings—that is, flat wings—and a tail rudder

that consisted of two plane kites intersecting at right angles. This was "the first true airplane in history."

As a boy, Cayley had put together a kind of kite that was really a helicopter. As a man, he put together planes that were really a kind of kite—gliders. Of a glider that he made in 1818, he wrote: "A child's kite furnishes a good experiment on the balancing and steering of aerial vehicles. . . ." And indeed, his plane was little more than a 154-square-inch kite mounted on a rod with a tail at the rear. But Cayley was a man slightly ahead of his time. No power unit had yet been invented that was compact enough to give the glider the necessary thrust to transform it into a real airplane.

Meanwhile, the men playing with man-lifting kites were taking the attention away from the gliders.

Captain Dansey and Father Cordner were patenting their giant kites for rescue work.

In 1876, Joseph Simmons was drawn into the air some 600 feet by two kites. Then, using guy lines, he glided to earth. He filed a patent for his kite invention as an "improved means and apparatus for conveying or carrying human beings or objects into mid-air."

By 1894, Lord B. F. S. Baden-Powell of England was building kites thirty-six feet high and flying military observers for the British Army.

For a while, the initial impetus that Cayley had given to airplane design was all but forgotten.

Then the Australian Lawrence Hargrave built a *better* kite, and the air race was on.

Hargrave's role—and the role of the kite—in airplane history cannot be overstated. In fact his likeness, with a background of kites and airplanes, is on the new Australian twenty-dollar bill, so highly is his work thought of! What Hargrave built was the first box kite.

The box kite embodied Hargrave's revolutionary principle of "cellular construction of kites." It was simple. It was

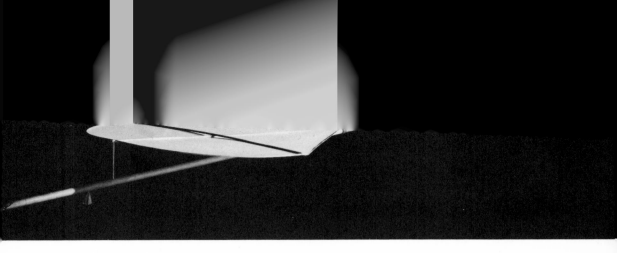

Sir George Cayley's glider, "the first true airplane in history," was little more than a 154-square-inch kite mounted on a rod with a tail at the rear.

The first men to fly were those who used kites to pull themselves aloft. In fact, man-lifting military kites similar to these led directly to man's conquest of the air.

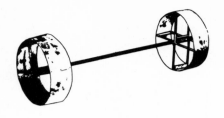

These are a few of the many different cellular kites Lawrence Hargrave experimented with before coming up with the now-classic box kite.

unique. And it was the basis for the famous Wright brothers' flights at Kitty Hawk.

What Lawrence Hargrave did was to find out how birds soared *without* flapping their wings. His first attempt at a rigid structure was a cellular kite which he described as resembling "two pieces of honeycomb put on the ends of a stick." His was a search for stability. By 1894, Hargrave was being lifted by a train of four cellular kites, with an anemometer in one hand, and a clinometer in the other. His experimental devices were not patented, for Hargrave was a dedicated scientist who felt that his inventions and aeronautical discoveries belonged to the world.

And so they did. The French inventor Gabriel Voisin

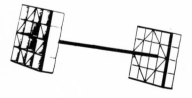

began experimenting with the new cellular kites (he called them "Hargraves") in 1895. At first they were toys to him, toys that grew progressively larger and larger. Finally, flying one enormous Hargrave in a thunderstorm, Gabriel and his brother Charles were lifted into the air by the wind-whipped kite. It started the Voisin brothers thinking about

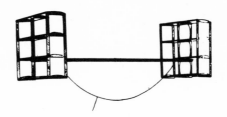

flying machines. That thinking led them to construct a box-kite-like glider on floats, the true ancestor of the European biplane.

While the Voisin brothers were flying their Hargraves in France, another pair of brothers were experimenting with kites and gliders in America—Wilbur and Orville Wright.

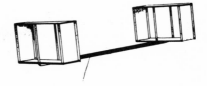

They, too, began by making box kites and studying wind and air currents. (Their Kitty Hawk biplane was really a box kite with wings three times as long as its body.) The Wright brothers selected Kitty Hawk on the North Carolina coast because it was a place where there were strong winds almost every day.

Lying on the center of the bottom wing of their box-kite glider, Wilbur hung on for dear life. Orville, holding the strong line, ran downhill. The kite bumped over the sand, rose into the air, glided a few feet, and nosed into the ground. Wilbur tumbled off, more out of breath than hurt. But the Wright brothers had begun.

Alexander Graham Bell, inventor of the telephone, also tried to invent the airplane, and so he experimented with many kinds of kites, some of which he exhibited in St. Louis in 1904.

Of course Wilbur and Orville Wright built more gliders and more kites and eventually put a motor into one of them until finally, on December 17, 1903, the "Air Age" was born.

Later Voisin combined the Wright brothers' design with the Hargrave structure for a tail, and became the first professional aircraft manufacturer in the world. In June 1905, on the Seine, a motorboat towed such a machine and in July of the same year Voisin and Louis Blériot produced another float-glider. These two planes were the first practical application of the box kite in full-scale aviation.

Meanwhile, in America, further kite experiments were

being performed by the inventor of the telephone, Dr. Alexander Graham Bell. He was working with man-lifting kites over forty feet long, kites often described as being "as big as a barn."

In 1903, Bell wrote, "I have had the feeling that a properly constructed flying machine should be capable of being flown as a kite; and conversely, that a properly constructed kite should be capable of use as a flying machine when driven by its own propellers." And Bell so experimented with kites of various shapes from 1898–1910. He wanted to discover a flying machine that could both hover— that is, move up and down for safe ascent and descent— and also move horizontally. In order to do this, he set about developing a kite that would be strong and light, stable, and

In 1908, with photographers present to record his successes, Bell sent up one of his multicellular kites from Cape Breton Island in Nova Scotia.

"Big as a barn" was the description of Bell's giant tetrahedal kites, one of which carried a man 168 feet in the air. Shown here is Dr. Bell helping his team with one of his monster kites.

provided with propellers. He began with the Hargrave kite which he called the "high-water mark of progress in the nineteenth century." Bell's contribution to kites and to the story of aviation was the tetrahedral kite, that is, a cellular kite in which the cells are triangular in shape.

By 1905, Dr. Bell had created his first man-lifter, the *Frost King*. The *Frost King* was made of 1300 tetrahedral cells, each ten inches to a side. It had a rope ladder from which a man could be suspended. By 1907, the *Cygnet* was completed, 3,393 cells big. In its center was an opening for a man to sit. On December 6, 1907, launched from a steamer in Baddeck Bay in Nova Scotia, the *Cygnet* carried Lieutenant Thomas E. Selfridge of the U. S. Army 168 feet high in the air for seven minutes. Unfortunately, the lineman on the boat was not quick enough and when the kite descended, he allowed it to drag through the bay where it was destroyed. Lieutenant Selfridge escaped with only a soaking and went on, ironically, to become a victim of the first air-age disaster. He was killed in the crash of an early Wright biplane in Fort Myer, Virginia, in September 1908.

At the same time that Bell, Voisin, and the Wrights were at work on their kites and gliders, another man was experimenting with biplane-kite-gliders in England—Samuel Franklin Cody. A Texas-born American, he was the first man to fly in England.

Learning about kites from the Chinese cook on the Cody ranch, young Samuel was in love with the idea of flying from his childhood. However, he imitated Buffalo Bill Cody and went touring through Europe in a Wild West Show. All the while, though, he toyed with aerial science.

Cody's first manned air flight took place on a hillside in North London, using kites in tandem tethered to a wire cable that was secured to a winch. Cody was lifted eighty feet into the air but a sudden gust of wind made the kites dive into the trees. Cody managed to save his life by hanging on to the upper branches of the trees and vowed, as he swung there, to redesign the kites. He did so, using four to six kites to lift a cable which in turn lofted the man-lifter. To the large man-lifter, Cody affixed a two-wheeled

Mr. Cody successfully lofted one of his new kites.

Interested in aerial science, Mr. Cody experimented with kites of different shapes.

pulley. To the pulley he attached a small basket seat. Bridle lines controlled the ascent and a brake fitted to a pulley block would lock into place if the man on the kite wanted to observe the area or take photographs. Cody was so pleased with his invention that he demonstrated it to the government at Plumstead. The government was not interested.

Cody did not give up his kite ideas, though. He made

In one experiment, Mr. Cody attached a kite to a boat.

Cody's kite-towed trip across the English Channel took him thirteen hours.

a kite-towed trip in a boat across the English Channel. It took him thirteen hours. In 1901 he patented a kite that had wing-warping for lateral control, a kite the Wright brothers incorporated in their own patent of 1903. Finally Cody worked on war kites. Then, at last, the government was interested.

Cody went from kite flying to become the first man to build and fly an airplane in England in a historic flight that took place in October 1908. Though months of further experiments followed, with frequent crashes and even more frequent ribbings from the local newspapers, S. F. Cody went on to build the now legendary *Flying Cathedral*. It was the largest airplane in existence at the time and he flew forty miles cross-country—a world record.

And so the kite led directly to the airplane.

But now the kite is leading further than that. It is pointing man to the stars too. The work of one man, Francis M. Rogallo, is as vital to the newest link between kites and flying as Lawrence Hargrave's box kite was nearly eighty years ago.

Rogallo, who is chief engineer of the 7 x 10-foot wind tunnels at Langley Air Force Base in Virginia, invented a flexible kite in 1941. It has no sticks or ribs or spars and

In the 7 x 10-foot wind tunnel at Langley Air Force Base, F. M. Rogallo checks the performance of one of his flexible kites.

Only recently tabled by NASA was an experiment using the Rogallo "parawing" (based on the flexible kite) to lower full-scale models of the Gemini capsule.

may be sat upon or stamped upon, or rolled up and put away in its wind-sock tail. It flies with shroud lines very much like a parachute and resembles nothing so much as the paper airplanes that sail riotously about in classrooms. And according to experts, it may very well be the fore-runner of flexible aircraft in the future.

The flexible kite, or Flexikite, came about because Rogallo wished to demonstrate an aspect of flight neglected in airplane design—the importance of flexibility to an airplane's maneuverability. Because the Flexikite is frameless,

The bat-winged "paraglider" (also based on the flexible kite) is maneuvered to a preselected landing site by a North American Aviation test pilot.

it can constantly adjust to changes in the force of the wind by changing its shape—something no other kite can do.

What does this mean in terms of airplanes and rocket flight? The airplanes of today began as rigid-framed box kites. They soon developed into man-carrying gliders. Next they were fitted with engines to provide them with motive power. In the hundreds of years of interest in the idea of air flight, aircraft design has come quite a long way from the original framed kite. But as far as it has come, it has never discarded the *principle* of the rigid frame. It is now centuries after the discovery of what scientists call the "rigid lifting surface." For the first time, Rogallo has offered the "non-rigid lifting surface." And the new experimenters, led by Rogallo's thinking, believe that the time may soon be at hand for applying this new principle to man-carrying gliders and from there to powered flexible aircraft.

58

The Rogallo Flexwing, according to its inventor, may one day be used in high-powered flight, and many experimental models using the flexible kite are being tested in NASA laboratories.

The Rogallo flexible kite itself has undergone changes since 1941 when it was first put together and tested in the Rogallo home. The Flexwing, based on Rogallo's patent, has been used by powerful aircraft companies like Ryan Aeronautical and North American Aviation. The Fleep has been built, a flying jeep which can lift loads up to a half-ton—a jeep that is equipped with a Flexwing. In March 1966 in Fort Bragg, North Carolina, the army's crack parachute team tested modified Flexikites as parachutes. And for a while, though it has recently been tabled, the Rogallo "parawing" was being used to lower full-scale models of Gemini capsules.

Rogallo hypothesizes that people may soon be flying high-powered planes built on the flexible-kite theory. It may be possible that these planes could crash without being destroyed. It is even conceivable that the flexible flying vehicle will be able to break through the so-called "thermal barrier," one of the final barriers in space. Although the rigid flying vehicle has been able to fly through the sound barrier, it has been unable to overcome the so-called "thermal barrier" because of the tremendous friction involved. This "barrier" is based on the scientific hypothesis that any rigid instrument builds up heat through friction at high speeds and that upon attaining maximum speeds the ordinary rigid plane would destroy itself by self-generated fire. However, the non-rigid flying machine—at least in theory—would not be consumed because it could change its shape and adapt to any and every aerodynamic situation.

A
Contract
of
Glory

From the air and airwaves to suspension bridges and advertising, kitestrings have tied many surprising packages for scientists and scholars. But far surpassing the kite's usefulness in things of this earth is the way the kite has represented man's link with God. For many millions of people in the world, the kite long stood for man's soul.

In Polynesia, which includes New Zealand and Micronesia, as well as the Hawaiian islands, kite flying grew up first as part of a religion. Rehua, the god of the highest heaven, often called the "sacred bird," was a kite flier, like the twin gods Rongo and Tane. The Hawaiians especially revered the demigod Maui, sometimes known as "the Hercules of Polynesia," whose favorite kite-flying field was by the boiling pools of the Wailuku River.

The Maori were great kite fliers and had special kite songs, called karakias, *which they sang while a small disk attached to the kitestring rose up to meet the bird-shaped kites.*

Kite flying was so much a part of the Polynesian religions that *karakias*, special kite songs, were sung as the kites ascended. Only the right hand was used for holding the kite line—the left was considered taboo. And special tribesmen were designated as the official kite fliers.

To the Polynesians, the kite was not a toy but a symbol of the soul of its owner. Often a chief was referred to in terms of the form of his kite the way a medieval knight was sometimes known by the color or shape of his crest.

Kite flying in northern, east central, and southern Polynesia was so important that it was taboo for a woman even to touch the kites. It was strictly a man's business, and usually priestly business at that. The priests, or *tohungas*, were the great kite fliers and used their kites as demon quellers. The *tohungas* were also the navigators on long canoe voyages because, with their knowledge of the winds gained from kite flying, they could tell all about the weather and the ocean currents.

In New Zealand, the Maori said: "The flying kite foretells a man's luck; if it swoops, it is bad luck, ominous; if it is steady, then truly the sun shines before." And in certain tribes, only the chiefs—or the greatest warriors dressed in the chiefs' special clothes of dogtails and white dogskins— were allowed to fly the sacred kites. Two men, one for holding the string and one for throwing the kite in the air, would set the kite flying. As it rose, the tribe would shout for joy. Then a small disk or messenger was attached to the string and, as it rose, the tribe sang the *karakia*:

> *Climb up! Climb up!*
> *To the highest surface of the heaven,*
> *To all the sides of heaven.*
> *Oh, thou,*
> *Extend thyself*
> *To the seventh division,*
> *To the eighth division,*
> *The world is made one with space.*
> *Where is the sacredness?*
> *The sacredness is in the tranquil temple,*
> *The spacious temple,*
> *"Holiness in the Heavens."*
> *Climb thou to thy ancestor, the sacred bird,*
> *To thy ancestor, Rehua in the heavens.*

The sacred kites were flown to foretell victory in times of war and forecast luck in times of peace. They were used to divine where to settle and also used as a means of settling quarrels. The Maoris used a special kind of kite, the *manu taratahi*, for this kind of divination. It was a diamond-shaped kite with projecting plumes.

Sometimes the *manu taratahi* was used as a crime-detector. When murder was suspected in connection with the death of a person, the kite was given the dead man's name. This tradition arose over four hundred years ago, when two young brothers were missing from their home. The unhappy mother finally consulted a priest, who decided to use two kites to discover the whereabouts of the missing boys. Each kite was

The bird shape of this Maori bird kite was often used. This usually signified the bringing of good fortune.

named after one of the boys and immediately flown. They rose steadily and then suddenly swooped toward a neighboring village. There they righted themselves and hovered over a single dwelling—the home of the chief. It soon came out that the chief had murdered the two boys and he was found guilty and quickly punished. Thus kite divination became firmly established in that area.

In Micronesia, on the island of Rathman, religious festivals honoring the sacred bird, the gannet, were held. Kites called after the gannet were flown because tradition held that from time to time the god commanded his worshipers

Maori kites were sometimes used for divination. These kites, known as manu taratahi, *had projecting plumes.*

to make a kite with a long tail and that the entire congregation was to attend its flying.

The Polynesian folk heroes, too, the demigods, were often great kite fliers. The Maoris spoke of Tawhaki who ascended to heaven as a kite to make war upon the god. As he rose, he chanted a kite song. But his wings were broken in battle and he fell to the earth.

The Hawaiians said that Maui—who was supposed to be the common ancestor of all the brown people of the Pacific—once made a kite larger than a house. But the kite rose too slowly for the impatient Maui, and he remembered

an old priest named Kaleiioku who owned a covered calabash. With this calabash, Kaleiioku could summon the
winds whenever he wished. So Maui traveled to Waipio
where the old priest lived and persuaded the old man to
lend him the calabash. Then Maui sang:

> *Oh, winds, winds of Waipio,*
> *In the calabash of Kaleiioku,*
> *Come from the calabash,*
> *Come quickly, come with power.*

And the winds came, roaring and surging. They ripped
the kite from Maui's hands and tossed it far over the vol-
canoes of Hawaii to the other side of the mountains. Angrily,
Maui leaped over the mountains to find his giant kite. But
when he finally caught up with it, his anger was abated
and ever after, according to the legend, he was more respect-
ful of the winds. And, too, the Hawaiians said that when
Maui died, his kite fell from the sky, landing far up on
the top of a mountain, where it may be seen until this
very day. And they point to a flat plot of land between
Mauna Kea and Mauna Loa which they call Maui's Kite.

In China, too, the flying kite was regarded as symbolic
of the human soul. The Chinese say, "The soul is like a
flying bird," and kites were thought to bring good luck.
Each kite in ancient China was especially decorated and
each decoration had a meaning. A kite sacred to a certain
god or warrior would carry his picture or symbol high up
toward the heavens.

The most famous of the Chinese religious kite festivals
took place on the ninth day of the ninth month and was
known as *Ch'ung-yang*, "The Festival of Climbing the
Heights" or "The Festival of Ascending On High." On
this day, until very recently, all manner of kites were flown
throughout the country, with figures of men and women,
of birds, of centipedes, of giant dragons or groups of fierce

An old drawing illustrates the most famous Chinese kite festival, The Festival of Climbing on High, when thousands of kite fliers took to the hills to loft their kites.

hawks. Some particularly interesting kites were made of bands of colored papers and were known as "women's robes." There were also singing kites that had strips of rawhide stretched taut on the bamboo frames. The wind played across these strips like a persistent violinist.

According to tradition, "The Festival of Ascending On High" began many centuries ago when a man was warned by a seer that on the ninth day of the ninth moon a great calamity would befall his house and all within. So that day he took his family and servants on an all-day picnic to the countryside where they spent their time flying kites. Upon their return, they discovered their house in ruins and their animals all killed by marauders. Thanking the gods for the warning, the man each year—with all his household—retired to the hills to picnic and fly kites on the same day.

The festival grew and grew until it was celebrated in almost all of China. In fact, every year there would be a special proclamation warning against the "tumult" caused by the thirty to forty thousand people who took to the hills that surround Canton to fly their kites. And a special mandarin and policemen were assigned to keep the peace there.

Another kite ceremony, known as "Driving Away the Devil" celebrated a Chinese boy's seventh birthday. At that time, his parents would make him a straw kite to carry away any evil that might surround him. The father lofted the kite and paid out all of the string. When the kite was at its highest point, the father let go of the string and the kite sailed off, bearing the evil with it.

A third ceremony involving a kite occurred when a farmer's son came of age. He was then presented with a "rice kite" to fly over his own paddies. A sheaf of rice dangled from each side of the kite and one from the tail, and as the kite was flown, the wind would shake loose the grains and sow them on the ground. If the farmer's son kept his kite aloft until the last grain was dropped, it was a sign of bountiful crops for the rest of his life.

Recent visitors to China, however, say that the religious kite festivals are no longer approved by the government. In fact, one statement from the interior warned against kites as a measure supported by counterrevolutionaries, citing how the electricity in one area had been cut off by a kitestring that sawed against a powerline.

Prayer kites were once very popular in ancient Korea and still may be found in parts of the countryside. Korean mothers wrote prayers on the kites asking that the evil of the year might be caught by the wind and made to vanish into the heavens. Then the kites were set free.

In Thailand, not only was the kite considered a man's soul, but the King of Siam had a special kite and a group of special kite mandarins. These men would take turns flying the king's kite all night long to keep his soul high and safe from the dark and evil night while his body lay below in sleep. At other times, large paper kites were sent up in the Thai countryside to help the crops grow by calling to the gods of wind and rain.

The Indian kites were not used as part of any specific religious ceremony. But Musailima, the false prophet who lived at the time of Mohammed, is said to have flown kites strung with musical bows. He sent them aloft at night and the wailing and humming sounded to his uneducated followers like the singing of angels. This was, of course, just as Musailima had planned and he claimed to be conversing with these angels while the people were sleeping.

Although kites were used as part of religious worship almost exclusively in the East, there are some instances of the practice in the western hemisphere also. The island of Bermuda adopted a schoolteacher's idea many years ago and to this day kites are flown on Good Friday as a sign of Christ's ascension into Heaven. Although the teacher's name has long since been forgotten, his story is retold every year. Trying to explain to his Sunday School class exactly what was meant by Christ's ascending into Heaven, he finally hit upon a simple plan. He took the class out to the beach on Good Friday and unfolded a large paper kite on which he had painted a picture of Jesus. Then he lofted the kite, to the delight of his class. When the kite had reached its maximum height, the teacher cut the string. The kite hovered for a minute over the beach, then slowly rose and disappeared into the sky, "ascending," as the teacher explained, "into Heaven." Good Friday kite flying has been a tradition in Bermuda ever since.

It is not surprising that the kite should be thought of as a symbol for man's soul. It is constructed of the crude materials of earth—of sticks and cloth and vines and paper. Yet it dares to fly up to the heavens where, traditionally in almost all religions, the gods or God dwells. What *is* surprising is that such a beautiful, gentle object of contemplation could also be turned into an instrument of war. Yet the kite was the forerunner of many of the weapons that can be found in any modern arsenal.

Bermuda is the scene of the only religious kite festival in the West. On Good Friday, kites are flown all over the island to symbolize the ascension of Christ.

The Kite in War

As early as 206 B.C. kites were linked with the world's battles. Han-Sin, one of the most famous generals of China, is among the first men of war to be associated with the kite. According to legend, Han-Sin was leading a rebel army that wanted to storm the palace of Wei-Yang-Kong and overthrow the cruel emperor. But the palace was well guarded by high walls and many soldiers. The rebel army could not take it by a direct attack for they were inferior in arms and men. If they were to have a chance, they had to come upon the emperor's stronghold by surprise.

Yet there seemed no way to creep up on the palace for it lay in the center of a great plain. Any invaders could be seen easily, even if they crept in from the surrounding hills. So, Han-Sin had to devise another way to gain entrance to the fortress. He decided to dig a tunnel from the hills that circled the plain, a tunnel that would go beneath the well-guarded walls. It was an excellent and daring plan, but it had one serious drawback. There was no way to measure the distance accurately. And a bad guess could cost Han-Sin too many men. It could even mean the defeat of the rebellion.

It was then that Han-Sin thought of using a kite. He built one of bamboo and cloth and sent it sailing high above the plain. When it was directly over the palace, he marked and measured the string. In this way, the rebels were able to calculate how long a tunnel they needed to dig to be well within the fortress walls. The trick worked. The wicked emperor was overthrown. And Han-Sin helped to put Liu Pang on the throne and to establish the famous Han dynasty that ruled China for over four hundred years.

During Liu Pang's reign, a kite was again used in war. This time, a musical bow strung with silk was attached to the kite and flown at night. Rebellious troops heard the sounds and interpreted them as "Fu Han," "Beware of Han," and they fled, fearing the spirits and the armies of Han equally.

Many centuries later, in Korea in A.D. 647 another kite took part in a rebellion. A certain General Yu-shin Kim was in charge of putting down rioters who rose against the government of Queen Jinduk of the Silla dynasty. One evening, when the fighting was at its worst, a giant meteor fell, lighting the sky with its fiery trail. The loyal troops were exhausted and looked upon this as a sign that the queen, too, was destined to fall. And so they were ready to give up. But General Kim was not a superstitious man and he realized that he would have to do something to put courage back into the hearts of his tired, failing men. So, late that night, when only a few men remained up on watch, the general built a giant kite and attached a lantern to its tail. As the kite ascended, the general sent word that the star was again rising, and that the gods were willing to forgive the troops their momentary fear. The believing soldiers took it as a good omen. Refreshed, they went on to defeat the rebels and saved Queen Jinduk's throne and the dynasty.

Similar tales can be found in Maori and Tahitian folk-lore. There, kites with firebrands attached were flown at night and these "fiery demons" spread dismay through the enemy ranks.

In a Maori battle ritual, when a force was ready to attack a fortified village or *pa,* the priest would make a special kite of the jointed stems of the sedge, which is a grasslike plant that grows in marshy places. The kite had to measure six feet from tip to tip and the line was of strips of un-dressed flax tied together. While the priest constructed the sedge kite, no member of the attacking force was allowed to eat or the spell would not work; the god of war, *Tu,* would not aid them.

When the kite was finished, if it flew lopsided, it meant disaster. But if the kite flew straight and true, it meant that *Tu* smiled upon the warriors and all would go well. Maybe.

While the sedge kite ascended, the *tohunga* recited a special charm called a *turu,* and only then were the hungry warriors allowed to eat. In fact, they were supposed to eat then, for during their feast, the priest had yet another duty to perform. He attached a "messenger" of woven leaves to the cord and the wind blew it up to the kite. When the messenger reached its goal, the *tohunga* released the line and liberated the kite. Then the warriors stopped their feasting and watched with fear and awe as the kite made its way toward the enemy village.

If the *tohunga* launched the kite properly, on the wind-ward side of the town to be taken, the drifting cord would trail over the enemies' land. And if by mistake or mischance any man, woman, or child in the enemy village caught hold of the line, the warriors would shout with joy for that was the best sign of all that the village would surely be taken.

But an ironic thing about the kite ceremony of the Maoris was that, in many cases, the people of the *pa* would not be aware that they were about to be attacked until they saw the magic kite fly over their land. Thus the kite often gave them a warning and just those few moments were enough for them to prepare for battle.

The Maoris were not merely superstitious in their use of kites. They could be practical and as inventive as the Chinese General Han-Sin. Over two hundred years ago, one chief named Nuku-pewapewa tried to take a village known as Maunga-rake. The village was not only well fortified but surrounded by cliffs as well. Nuku decided to use a giant bird-shaped kite to lower a man from an adjacent cliff at night. That man opened the gateway of the *pa* to the attackers and, before morning, Maunga-rake was taken.

In the twelfth century, Korea, too, used men on kites in war. A certain General Yong Cho was sent to one of the islands to put down a rebellion of Mongolian livestock farmers. When the army finally reached the coast, they found the rebels—like the Maori villagers—based on steep, impregnable cliffs. But the general launched large numbers of kites from his boats. To some of the kites he attached flaming torches and he maneuvered the kites above the rebels. Then he ordered the strings which bound the torches to the kites cut. A rain of fire descended on the villagers. Other kites carried General Cho's best archers. Once above the rebel stronghold, the archers shot their arrows down upon the startled farmers. This is perhaps the earliest known instance of an air attack.

Similar to the Korean flame throwers is a story told in

India of a kite used in war. In 1662, the fort of Chakan that sat upon a mountain peak in India was captured by a Mogul General Shaistekhan. He managed to explode its powder arsenal with a torch attached to a kite's tail.

The first recorded instance of a "leaflet raid" is found in the thirteenth-century war between the Chin Tatars and the Moguls. At a siege of Khaifeng in 1232, the besieged troops sent up kites with messages attached. When these came near the camps where the enemy kept its prisoners, the strings were cut. The messages floated out and the instructions told the prisoners to rise up, escape, and help the besieged town.

The Fiji islanders had yet another wartime use for kites. A besieged town flew its kite as a signal of pride, a kind of flag of courage. When an enemy approached, a circular kite of palm leaves decorated with white and colored ribbons made from mulberry bark was raised. The kite cord passed through a hole made in the top of a forty-foot pole that was set up in a conspicuous part of town. In this way, the floating banner could be raised and lowered as a colorful sign of defiance.

The early history of the kite in war is spotty, full of interesting anecdotes and adventures, but nothing more. Except for the Maori kite ritual—and no one knows for sure how old it is—the kite was for a long time far from being considered a conventional weapon of war—frequently useful, perhaps, but not to be relied upon. But, by the eighteenth century, as part of the preparation of man's final conquest of the sky, the Oriental war kite had become a regular piece of army equipment.

In Japan in the 1700s a kite large enough to swing a man in the air, a man seated in a kind of boatswain's chair, was not an unusual sight. Such flying observers spied out the location and arrangements of the enemy's troops and equipment. These kites, however, required strong winds

This miniature painting of a kite-balloon is from the 1405 manuscript by Konrad Kyeser von Eichstadt—one of the few early references to kites in Western military lore.

for they were from six to fifteen feet high, from four to ten feet wide, with a wind surface of up to 150 square feet. Usually these war kites were equipped with seven bridle lines and were attached to a stout rope on a winch that was driven into the ground and lashed as though to tent pegs.

The kite did not really enter Western battles until the

time of the Boer War, though the flying wind sock had been pictured as an oddity by the war technician Konrad Kyeser von Eichstadt in 1405. There it is shown as a kind of medieval banner or signaling device in which a rider holds a kite-balloon on a string. The kite is shaped like a dragon, the head of parchment and the body of linen, the tail of silk. A small oil lamp in the dragon's mouth warmed the air inside the body and supposedly lifted the kite-balloon into the air.

And even earlier, in 1326, an unfinished sketch in Walter de Milemete's treatise *De nobilitatibus, sapientiis, et prudentiis regum* showed a beleaguered town with a kite flown above it. From the kite hangs a bomb or fireball. The kite is held by three knights. However, unbeknownst to the

The Milemete manuscript of 1326 has an unfinished sketch which is the earliest known representation of aerial attack and defense, the bombs being carried aloft by kites.

diligent knights, a similar kite-suspended bomb hangs heavily over their own heads and the string for that kite comes from a house within the city! This is the earliest known pictorial representation of aerial attack and defense.

Nearly six centuries passed before the Western nations took up kite flying as a serious part of their war effort. Although kites were being flown scientifically from the middle of the eighteenth century on, it was not until 1894 that the Englishman B. F. S. Baden-Powell, brother of the founder of the Boy Scouts, gave kite flying its place in Western military history.

Captain Baden-Powell was a member of the Scots Guard when he built a kite thirty-six feet high—as high as a telephone pole, some people said. He built it that large in order to lift a man as a flying observer as the Japanese had done fully a century before. Balloon observers had been employed by the Western powers already, for exactly one hundred years. But they were really not very successful. For one thing, the balloons were easy targets, and a bullet hole in a balloon is a disaster. For another, the bulky balloons were entirely unmanageable in heavy winds and almost as unmanageable on the ground. And they were very expensive to maintain. Kites seemed the perfect solution.

Baden-Powell's kite was demonstrated to the British Army officials at Pirbright Camp near Aldershot, England, on June 27, 1894, and it so impressed them that flying observers on kites became an integral part of their Boer War operations several years later.

But by the time of the Boer War, Baden-Powell had discarded the single kite in favor of six smaller kites flown in tandem. He ascended as high as one hundred feet, pulled aloft by his six hexagonal kites. These giant twelve-by-twelve-footers could raise a man even in dead calm, for they had a retaining line fixed to a wagon that towed the kites along.

Baden-Powell also saw in the kite possibilities for carrying messages from ship to ship. From the deck of the destroyer *H.M.S. Daring*, Baden-Powell sent a package of secret letters to another ship nearby. He let out enough line so that the documents should fall aboard ship. Unfortunately, he miscalculated. The secret packages missed the ship entirely. Luckily, the kite lines fell across the deck and an alert crew pulled the letters from the sea, wet but otherwise unharmed.

Two years after the Pirbright demonstration, Lieutenant Hugh D. Wise, an American, built a large kite to show the United States Army how useful winged observers would be. He used a giant kite that was pulled aloft by three smaller kites. Then Lieutenant Wise entered a boatswain's chair attached to the main line and was sent aloft some forty-two feet. Lieutenant Wise wrote of his flight that it "was not at all unpleasant—a gentle swaying and lifting not unlike the motion of a swing." This was in January of 1896.

In 1898, when the U.S. was involved in the Spanish-American War, hundreds of photos were taken with kite-flown cameras.

By the time of the Boer War (1899–1902), kites were used not only for flying observers but also for signaling and photo reconnaisance as well. And, hypothetically at least, they had been suggested for "dropping bombshells upon the enemy . . . by releasing the bomb by electricity" which was to be conveyed by a light cable instead of a kite rope.

Samuel Cody, who did so much for early air flight, was also interested in the military uses of kites. And the military finally became interested in him. The British Admiralty Commission invited Cody to demonstrate his man-hauling kites on Whale Island in Portsmouth, and he dutifully went there one fine Sunday morning in 1903. He first sent his son Vivian aloft two hundred feet to take photographs. Then Cody himself ascended four hundred feet.

Cody's man-lifting war kites were adopted by the British army in 1906. Here he demonstrates their maneuverability for the military by sending several men up the side of an otherwise unscalable mountain.

Next his other son, Leon, rose eight hundred feet on a kite and took photographs of the warships in the harbor. This was, to all intents and purposes, the birth of the Royal Air Force. The next year, Cody was engaged by the War Office to experiment with kites for artillery observation and photo reconnaissance. He became attached to the balloon factory at Farnborough, Hants. And finally, in 1906, S. F. Cody achieved what was the first really official "title" in Western kite history. He was appointed Chief Kite Instructor to the British Army and took over a special workshop at Crystal Palace in London.

Not to be outdone, the Germans, too, began to use kites in the early 1900s. The aeronautics division of the German army adopted the balloon kite that recalled the experiments of von Eichstadt. Essentially this was a gasbag filled with hydrogen and flown like a kite. With it, the Germans were able to raise signal officers high enough to scrutinize the surrounding country.

It would seem that, with the beginning of modern airplanes, the kite's military uses would dwindle. And so they did—for a while. But by World War II, new military uses for the kites had been found. Two Americans—Paul Edward Garber and Harry C. Sauls—were responsible for the most outstanding of them.

The target kite was the invention of Commander Paul Garber, U.S.N.R., in response to a need that grew out of developing air flight. To train antiaircraft crews, some sort of target that was both realistic and maneuverable—and yet inexpensive—was necessary. Obviously real planes could not be used. They were much too expensive and besides the pilots were certainly not expendable. Balloons were in use at the time, but again they were expensive, bulky to stow, and about as hard to miss as a flying barn.

The kite that Commander Garber invented was five feet square, and had a rudder for control. It could be made to

A kite balloon showing a United States Army crew before the release of handling lines at Fort Monmouth, New Jersey.

move like an enemy plane—loop, dive, zoom, and execute figure eights. An outline of the enemy plane was painted on the surface and, at 150 yards, the silhouette resembled a plane at a distance of about a mile. In flight, the blue cloth merged into the sky, and the picture of the plane stood out convincingly. About a half million of these kites were made and used widely throughout the American fleet and at shore stations. And though kites were eventually replaced by radio-controlled gasoline model airplanes, a Navy source says that they are still practical for elementary instruction with small-caliber machine guns.

While Commander Garber was at work on his target kite, Harry Sauls was busy testing his own invention—a barrage kite. The barrage kite was used to remove the terror of enemy planes that swooped out of the skies to make a strafing run across the deck of a ship. A series of

The target kite, shown here by the inventor, Commander Paul Garber, was a realistic and maneuverable target to train anti-aircraft crews.

kites flown with heavy wires stretched tightly between them would entangle the aircraft in their lines. The kites that Sauls created looked like small biplanes or gliders, and could quickly be erected on the deck of a ship and launched from the stern. In this way, they kept the bombers at bay. Again, balloons had been used for barrage purposes before the invention of the Sauls kite, but the same objections were always found. Balloons were bulky, difficult to inflate, excellent targets for the guns of the enemy, and expensive to replace.

Harry Sauls's kites were first tested in Chesapeake Bay on January 12, 1943, from the Maritime Commission's training ship *American Navigator*. They were so successful that they were used regularly thereafter to protect North Atlantic convoys en route to Europe with war materials.

Besides the target kite and the barrage kite, the Allied

Harry C. Sauls, the inventor of the barrage kite, stands next to one of his creations which were used in World War II to entangle enemy airplanes making strafing runs on Allied ships.

armed forces in World War II found other uses for kites. Rigged with metal, kites were sent up as practice targets for radar trainees. RAF life rafts carried kites as standard equipment. If a pilot were forced down, he could manage to get his cotton-and-aluminum-tubing kite flying in a light wind. At a height of three hundred feet, the kite trailed a foil tail that enabled radar to plot the point where the pilot had bailed out.

Kites were standard American life raft equipment, too, but with a difference that has already been noted. They were used to loft SOS radio antennae.

But surely the strangest of all the war kites was the German "Sandpiper" invented for submarine observation by the German aircraft expert Heinrich Focke. It was a

84

combination kite and helicopter that could be taken apart or put together in seven minutes. The Sandpiper was a helicopter because it had rotor blades and a pilot's seat. But it had no motor and flew at the end of a rope and so was officially considered a kite. It weighed 180 pounds— without a pilot.

Two hundred of these flying periscopes were made by the German Weser Flugzeugwerke, and they were part of the equipment of many German submarines. When a U-boat had surfaced and wanted to scan the horizon for Allied ships, the pilot and his Sandpiper were sent aloft, connected to the submarine both by the towing cable that was attached to a winch on the ship's deck and by a direct-line telephone. Usually there was time to wind in the Sandpiper before the submarine made its dive. But in emergencies, when the kite could not be reeled in fast enough, the pilot released an emergency handle and the kite-helicopter sailed away free, with its hapless observer. And all that the Sandpiper pilot had in the way of an emergency pack then was a parachute and a prayer, which is a kind of roundabout return to the way in which kites began.

Variations on a Theme

In the hundreds of years that kites have existed, they have undergone many changes in form. First there were simple kites such as the Malay leaf kites, then more and more exotic Oriental fish and dragon designs. The complex box kite and Bell's tetrahedral kite came in the nineteenth century. And finally the "kytoon" and the flexible kite appeared.

Kite flying, too, has undergone change; there has been a change in the *use* of kites. We have seen it range from mystery and magic to war and science, back and forth through the ages.

But kite flying as a sport also has been transformed. And there are many variations on the simple theme of a kite and a piece of string. Often another element, the element of danger, has been added. More often, kite flying has been combined with another sport and fascinating hybrids are the result.

Now there are kites for fighting and kites for fishing. Water skiting is becoming a popular competitive game. There are many other variations of kiting. Every day, it seems, new kite fliers come up with new variations. While dedicated fliers need only a simple kite and a long ball of string to make them happy, the variations are interesting additions to the ancient sport.

Kite fighting is probably the most widespread of the variations. It is practiced in many countries, from the flat-topped roofs of India to the hillsides of Japan; from the palace grounds of Thailand to the beaches of Brazil.

There are basically three kinds of fighting kites. One type uses abrasive string, another a kind of fishhook attached to the bridlelines, and the third a knifelike tail. All three types of kites are easy to maneuver but should be handled only by expert fliers.

In India, kite fighting with abrasive string has been so carefully cultivated, it is definitely no longer an amateur's sport. There are professional kitemakers who devote their lives entirely to producing truly balanced kites for fighters. The kite fighters keep dozens of kites "hangared" in dust-proof, moth-proof boxes and have favorites they bring out for special occasions.

The Indian fighter kite is simple in appearance but it is actually designed with great subtlety. A brilliantly colored paper is stretched over curved and tapered bamboo sticks. The paper has been scored with a seashell to prevent it from crinkling in flight. As simple as the Indian fighter kite looks, it is a masterpiece of aeronautics. It is so delicately balanced that it can fly in the slightest breeze.

The line of the Indian kite is in two sections: the regular string, usually white, and the brightly colored

The Indian fighter, deceptively simple in appearance, is a carefully designed and balanced kite made of colored paper stretched over curved and tapered bamboo sticks.

cutting string. The cutting string is coated with powdered glass so that it can saw across the opponent's line with ease. This string—about 150 to 200 feet long—is attached to the kite's bridle, then broken off, and the regular string is attached to its end.

When the fighter kite lifts into the air above the Indian roofs, it is a bright challenge to fight. Soon another kite rises to meet it. Then the sport begins. The two kites dip and soar according to the wishes of their handlers. The object is to maneuver the cutting string of your kite across your opponent's white cord and saw it in two. The losing kite sails off into the unknown while the winner swings into a victory salute that begs to be challenged by another fighter.

The second kind of fighter is found in Thailand, where

kite fighting is a competitive sport with an umpire, fans, and even a special system of betting. National contests are held in the capital city of Bangkok in the large open space in front of the walled Royal Palace. King Mongkut, the ruler made famous in *Anna and the King of Siam* and *The King and I,* is credited with organizing the first official Thai kite fight during his nineteenth-century reign. Ever since then, the King and Queen of Thailand officially open the kite-fighting season by flying the first kite.

There are two kites in each contest, a big *Chula,* the male kite, and the smaller *Pakpao,* the female. They are both made of a tough paper stretched on bamboo frames. The *Chula,* though, is about seven feet high and roughly star-shaped with five points. Tied high on its cord are three bamboo barbs that are used to catch the line or tail of the female kite. And it is so strong, it needs a team of ten men to fly it. The *Pakpao,* on the other hand, is diamond-shaped and only thirty-four inches long, with a tail of starched cotton cloth. It is much lighter and easier to handle. It has a hook dangling beneath its neck.

The object of the Thai contest is for one kite to catch, obstruct, or entangle the other, making it lose its balance and plunge to the ground. The *Chula* tries to do this by force with its heavier weight and hooks. The *Pakpao* must use strategy, outmaneuvering the male and causing it to entangle itself.

The *Chula* is flown at critical moments by the team captain. If a catch is made, the captain snaps a brass pulley onto the string and, to the rhythm of his whistle, the male kite is reeled in with its prey. But if instead the *Pakpao* throws her hook around the *Chula* or causes it to lose its balance, the captain's whistle shrills faster and faster as the desperate team tries to bring its kite safely home.

Because the odds are with the heavier kite, the men who take bets in the crowd give two-to-one odds on the

Kite flying in Bangkok is a spectator sport in which the crown bets on its favorite, whether it is the diamond-shaped Pakpao *or the larger star-shaped* Chula.

Pakpao; that is to say, someone placing a bet knows that a winning female kite is worth twice as much as the male. And the crowd cheers wildly for its favorite. If the *Pakpao* wins, often the exuberant fans will lift both the kite and its handler to their shoulders and parade them through the streets.

Some of the expert Thai fighting kites cost from fifty to

seventy-five dollars. But considering the money that is changing hands in the crowd while the kites are fighting, this is not very much at all.

A less commercial but equally enthusiastic kind of kite fighting goes on in Japan. It dates back to the 1570s when the Portuguese sailors introduced kite fighting to the southern island of Kyushu.

Spring has come to mean the time of kite fights on the hills overlooking Nagasaki. Although the abrasive string—the Japanese call it *biduro*—is sometimes used, the Japanese also employ several knives for the tail of the kite. They are made from short pieces of bamboo slit lengthwise in several places with curved blades of metal or glass inserted in the slits.

This is not the one-to-one kind of combat of the Indian or Thai kite fights. The Kyushu fights are mass rallies where the object is to cut down as many rivals as possible.

The air is filled with many colorful kites each spring as the Japanese boys compete with one another below, the kites with one another above. When a defeated kite flies off, many avid spectators pursue it. Such a kite belongs to anyone who captures it, just as a baseball goes to the fan in the bleachers who gets to it first. In fact, spectators often carry long bamboo poles to help them retrieve kites from the trees.

Many years ago, the kite fights were family affairs, and there was much honor attached to the family that won the most fights in a day. It was so important that a family might enlist its servants, as well as sisters, brothers, and cousins to fly kites, bringing as many as one hundred kites onto the field. These kites were identified by a special family color or crest.

The Nagasaki fights were so popular that once, in 1781, the governor of the city prohibited them because the crops were being ruined by contestants running over the newly

Each spring the air is filled with kites in Japan. These men with their ceremonial dress are participating in a kite meet.

seeded ground. But the governor was less popular than the kite fights. They survived. He didn't.

More recently, kite fighting has been transplanted to South America. There, on the beaches of Brazil, a more dangerous method is practiced. The fighters stud their kites' wingtips with razor blades and slash at their opponents' kites; the battling kites often are cut to ribbons.

Kite fishing probably originated in Polynesia. And as late as World War II, the Solomon Islanders sailed out in canoes, carrying palm-leaf kites with them. From the kites hung nets made of strong spider webs which were slowly drawn along the water to entangle long-headed gar fish.

Boys compete with each other on the ground; their kites compete with one another in the air.

A thirty-two-by-twelve-inch fishing kite from the Solomon Islands is displayed in the British Museum.

In many of the Indonesian and Melanesian islands a slightly different form of kite fishing once existed. Bait and snare, rather than nets, were attached to the kite. And the kite itself was often flown from a rod rather than held by hand. In Java, the line was even fixed through a hole in a plank of the canoe. This arrangement, naturally, was better for deep-sea fishing where the pull of a large fish is often too strong for a single fisherman.

But as powerful boats and sophisticated fishing rigs replaced simple canoes, the kite gradually disappeared as basic fishing equipment in the island cultures. It is only recently that

Kite fishing is an old Polynesian sport brought up to date in the West where it is practiced off jetties and piers.

kite fliers in the West have become interested once again in kite fishing as a sport. They call it "skip fishing" and practice it from the beaches and jetties rather than from boats.

First the kite is cast into the air from a regulation fishing rod. The line is paid out until the kite is some 150 to 200 feet across the water. Then the line is locked into

A bite! The reeling begins. While the kite remains in the sky, the fish is brought onto shore.

place while the fisherman attaches the leader that carries both bait and weight. Finally the line is sent out again until it hovers over the spot where the fisherman thinks the fish are waiting.

Fishing is not the only water sport that has adopted the kite—swimming and water skiing have, too.

Benjamin Franklin's kite flying was not limited to his famous electricity experiment. As a boy he lay on his back in a pond and let his kite draw him along "in a very agreeable manner."

Kite swimming is at least as old as Benjamin Franklin. He wrote of the time when, as a boy, he tied his kite string to a stick. Then he lay on his back, held on to the stick, and was "drawn along the surface of the water in a very agreeable manner . . . without the least fatigue, and with the greatest pleasure imaginable."

A more modern group of swimmers, donning goggles and snorkel equipment, have been towed about the water by a high-flying kite. That way, there is scarcely a ripple to disturb the fish.

A more organized new kite sport is water skiting. The water skiter rides his kite high above a water course while being towed by a motorboat. In the last few years, this sport has grown so much that the American Water Ski Association has organized competitions and there are rigid rules which govern the meets. A rating system has been established to classify fliers according to ability—first class, expert, or master.

Giant two-frame kites are used in water skiting. They have trapeze bars slung underneath. It is the bar that supports the flier and carries the kite line.

In the early days of water skiting, the flier had to hang from the bar alone, and this made it necessary for anyone trying this sport to be very acrobatic and strong. Now, however, there are seatlike harnesses attached to the center of the bar with a quick-release mechanism in case of trouble.

The water skiters are towed by a motorboat which runs into the wind. Then, as the boat increases its speed, the kite—and flier—become airborne.

The water-skiting course, according to Jack Wylie, one of the original skiters, is divided into two sections: tricks and slalom. The slalom is similar to a regular ski run. It is a race against time through a zigzag course. The zigzag, in this case, is set by six buoys, staggered three on each side of the boat. There is a system of high water spouts that jet from the buoys around which the water skiter must fly. The slalom is an elimination event. First the rope length from the boat to the kite is set at 130 feet. Each time a water skiter makes a successful pass through the water spouts in the allotted time, his rope is shortened by thirty feet.

For the trick flying, each contestant is allowed two tries of twenty seconds apiece. The moment the kite becomes airborne, the skiter releases his water skis so that he can perform his trapeze tricks as easily as possible. There, twenty to eighty feet above the water, he hangs by his knees, swings, does headstands and handstands on the bars—as many and as varied a collection of tricks in the twenty seconds as he can do. The judges watch and mark each performance from a towboat or from boats that run ahead of the kite.

Records on water skites have been set, too. On September 19, 1965, two Frenchmen—Jacques Gafreville and Bernard Danis—crossed the English Channel on the kites in sixty-five minutes. They were 100 feet above the water.

Kiting partridge was a sport in nineteenth-century England. Hunters used a hawk-shaped kite and flew it over the fields. The partridge believed the kites to be real birds of prey. Therefore they stayed on the ground as the hunter approached rather than flying off. However, for a *real* hunter, there was something unsportsmanlike about this. As a certain Lord Onslow wrote: "It's poor sport, only good for getting a few birds for the pot."

Samuel Cody, the airplane inventor in Britain, also tried a kind of hunting with a kite. He used his kite to tow a boat upstream, intending to shoot wild duck. But the ducks, like the partridge, thought the kite was a hawk and refused to fly. Finally Cody and his sons had to raise them by reeling in the kites and shouting.

Sending messages by means of a kite goes back at least as far as the Chinese wars of 549 when the Emperor Wu, besieged in the city of Nanking, signaled his army officers of his plight.

Perhaps even older are the Maori tales of message-sending, for they are undated stories handed down in the oral tradition. According to one narrative, a certain chief had two wives who did not get along. But the second wife was younger and more beautiful, so the chief marooned his first wife on an island. There she gave birth to a son. She had very little food and small hope for survival, but she ate what she could from the bushes and trees and walked the beaches in search of anything that might have washed ashore. One day, the marooned wife was cooking

The Great Mogul period of Indian art is full of paintings in which sloe-eyed girls send up kites with messages for their lovers.

her meager meal when a kite dropped near her fire. It was a kite she recognized. It had been made by her brothers who were searching for her. Seeing the smoke from her cookfire, they had maneuvered their kite as close as they could to the source of the smoke. The marooned sister,

99

with charcoal from the fire, wrote a message on the kite and sent it back aloft. The brothers soon found the island and rescued her and her infant son.

When the chief saw that she was alive and well, he wanted her to return. He had, in her absence, decided that he preferred her to his young, flighty bride. But the brothers and the first wife were not convinced. They left the faithless chief to his own fate and lived, if not happily ever after, at least fairly well.

Another kind of kite message developed in India. Since Indian custom forbade young men to look upon or talk to unwed maidens, they sent love notes and small presents across palace walls on the tails of bright-colored kites. There the young girls would attach messages of their own and send the kites back again. There are many lovely paintings from the Great Mogul period of Indian art showing these sloe-eyed girls on the flat roofs with their kites.

A third kind of message sending was started by the target-kite inventor, Paul Garber. He used to fasten the strings of high-flying kites to logs near his home on Chesapeake Bay. Pasted to each kite was a message and a self-addressed post card. Sometimes the logs were towed many miles before the kites came down. Then anyone finding the kite would read Garber's message. It said that the finder could keep the kite but to please return the postcard telling where the kite finally ended its log-pulling journey.

A fourth kind of message sending can be done by any modern-day kite flier. Simply write a note on a piece of paper. Then cut a small hole in the paper and tear or cut the paper from the hole to the paper's edge. Slip the kite-string through the hole and push the message as far up the string as possible. The wind will nudge the message slowly up the string to the kite. There the changing breezes will tug at the paper, finally loosening it and sending it flying off on its own.

Messages, though, are not the only things that generations of kite fliers have learned to attach to their kites. The Chinese have always favored a musical kite. Credit for its invention is traditionally given to Li Yeh, a tenth-century kitemaker for the Chinese emperor, although musical kites have been mentioned in much earlier Chinese stories. Li Yeh took an ordinary paper kite and fastened a bamboo flute to its head. Then he flew the kite so that the wind struck the flute holes and produced sounds like a harp.

The Koreans have similar "wind harps" that make strange plaintive sounds. In Annam, along the South China Sea,

Credit for the musical kite is traditionally given to Li Yeh, a tenth-century Chinese kitemaker, who was the first to fasten a bamboo flute to an ordinary kite.

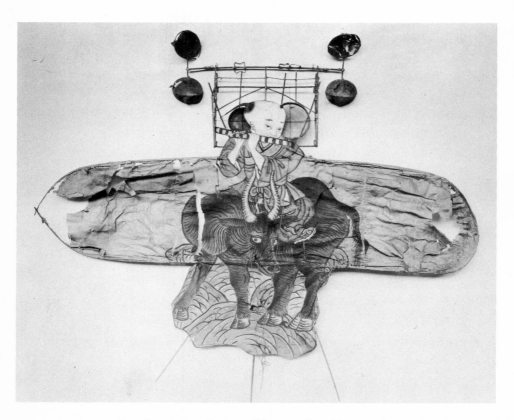

Another type of musical kite is this Chinese kite. The drum and cymbal at the top of the kite are struck by clappers activated by cups and cams rotated by the wind.

night kite flights are popular with a bamboo bow attached to the kites. The wind sings through the bow when the kite is aloft, playing a sad lullaby. In Peking, during the Manchu dynasty, this "Aeolian harp" was quite popular. The bow was often made of light willow wood as well as bamboo, and strung with silken threads. The Maori sometimes attached light fresh-water mussel shells to their kites. The shells rattled together in the wind.

Firecrackers, too, have been popular hitchhikers on kite-strings. The earliest kites in the West were, as John Bate wrote, merely the means to send "fier-works" into the air. But even before the seventeenth century the Oriental kite fliers had sent up firecrackers timed to explode when they reached certain heights.

Lanterns, flaming sticks, and flashlights have also ridden

The ABCD Kite Club of Terryville, Connecticut, display their giant 16 x 12-foot kite in 1887. From left: Burton Andrus, John Dieter, Leon Bunnell, Wallace Cook, and Arthur Bunnell.

Kite wagoners were among the most enterprising and engaging fliers, and the sport was known in the 1880s in America where the ABCD Kite Club told of nine-miles-an-hour trips.

on kite tails as military signals, signs, and finally as part of elaborate hoaxes. In 1887, the ABCD Kite Club of Terryville, Connecticut, lofted a lantern on their sixteen-by-sixteen-foot giant kite called *Skyscraper*. (The kite's tail itself was 104 feet in length!) They did it to frighten the neighbors at night. And they succeeded.

These days, there are stories of flying saucers that can sometimes be traced to kite fliers playing the game of UFO. By tying a two-celled metal flashlight to a kite and sending it up in the evening, these fliers have "created" unidentified flying objects (UFOs). In several instances, such flights have been specifically banned by law.

But perhaps some of the funniest variations were invented by kite wagoners. These enterprising fliers attached large kites to their carts, wagons, and other vehicles and were towed feet, yards, some even claimed miles, in one direction or another.

The ABCD club members, for example, attached a heavy clothesline to *Skyscraper* and tied it to a wagon. According to the *Bristol Herald*, the big kite towed a wagonload of rollicking members for an erratic miles-long ride. However, as a surviving club member remembers it, only one man was actually in the wagon as it was towed.

The Franklin Kite Club members wrote of being towed along the ice on the Delaware River on a kite-drawn sleigh one cold winter.

And Windwagon Smith, a frontiersman, is supposed to have crossed the Sea of Grass in a Conestoga wagon that was drawn by a giant kite after his horses were shot by Indians. Of such material tall tales are made.

But the most famous wagoning kite flier of all was George Pocock, the Bristol schoolmaster. His trip through the British countryside in the horseless carriage *Charvolant* deserves a special long look.

The Strangest Flights

Any activity with a history as long and as varied as kite flying is going to abound with unforgettable characters. Some of these are men and women who used the sport for their own publicity. Some are persons for whom kite flying was simply a means to some other end. Still others were kite fliers whose enthusiasm, fortunately or otherwise, knew no bounds. Of this last kind was George Pocock.

A schoolmaster in Bristol, England, in the early nineteenth century, Pocock had been a confirmed kite flier since childhood. As a boy he had used kites to tow small stones. Twenty-seven years later, as a teacher, he demonstrated to his pupils how kites hitched in tandem could draw a board along the road. One of his experimental kites, described earlier, was a precursor of the first airplanes.

Schoolmaster Pocock had a rather long-winded name for his kite-flying activities. He called it "aeropleustic art" and wrote an esoteric and almost unreadable book on the subject.

He also developed a special four-wheeled carriage which he planned to use in conjunction with two large circular kites. Pocock named his carriage *Charvolant*, using the French *char* or carriage and crossing it with *cerf-volant* which means kite. The two huge canvas kites that he called his "buoyant sails" were controlled by four lines. These lines or guide ropes were given the nautical names of "larboard and starboard traces" and used for avoiding the

George Pocock's kite-powered carriage, Charvolant, *managed to do twenty-five miles per hour in 1887, easily overtaking the London mail coach, but its "buoyant sails" caught on the trees.*

usual kite obstacles such as trees, church steeples, and the like. They were wound around a revolving spool. The carriage itself was steered by a T-shaped steering bar. The only way to stop *Charvolant* once it got going was by a brake which pressed a sharp iron into the earth. Inside the carriage were a mariner's compass and a clock.

On January 27, 1827, the graceful *Charvolant* journeyed the several miles between Bristol and Marlborough at twenty miles per hour, easily overtaking the London mail coach. But the longest single journey that George Pocock took in his lightweight carriage was a 113-mile trip across the British countryside. He was accompanied by two other such carriages each carrying several passengers, and they averaged twenty to twenty-five miles an hour for their trip.

Was Pocock the Henry Ford of kite fliers? Perhaps, though he was certainly not the first person to hitch a ride on a kite. As we have seen, countless trips had already been made on the wings of a kite, from the prehistory journeys of the Tahitian gods, through the Oriental war observers, up to the men of Pocock's own time—including his own son and daughter. But surely two of the strangest of these flights were made by a pair of Eastern desperadoes: one in China and another in Japan.

In China, during the Ming dynasty, when to look upon the Emperor's face unbidden meant death, an enterprising highwayman built a giant kite. One day, when the wind was right, he mounted the kite and was flown over the palace walls by his companions where he gazed upon the Emperor's face and was, in turn, seen by the Emperor. Before his friends could reel him in, the highwayman was captured by the Emperor's guards. He should have been beheaded but the Emperor was so amused and impressed by the man's daring and ingenuity that the highwayman was set free. Only his kite was confiscated. And the right of the common people to fly kites was immediately revoked.

At least, that is how the Chinese tell the tale. In Japan, a more documented story relates how a famous thief, Ishikawa Goyamen, wanted to steal two beautiful gold statues. The two statues, in the form of giant carp, adorned the top of a castle in Nagoya in central Japan, about 250 miles from Yokohama. The castle was the stronghold of a rich and powerful feudal warlord and at the time it was well guarded.

Goyamen could not hope to gain the golden fish by conventional means. Not only did he have to outwit the guards, he also had to manage to climb the many-tiered roof. So he waited until an exceptionally dark and stormy night. Then he and his confederates sent up several small kites that lofted a large kite over the castle. The large kite had, in place of a tail, a strong rope with a loop in which Goyamen could stand. In the storm, the rope tail swayed like a giant pendulum, but Goyamen was lifted onto the roof and reached the golden carp. The carp were worth a reputed five hundred thousand dollars—in the sixteenth century. But unfortunately the fish were much too heavy to be removed and all that the daring Goyamen was able to take was a few golden fins. For his trouble, Ishikawa Goyamen was boiled in oil, along with his entire family.

Some four hundred years later, another thief managed to remove fifty-eight scales from the famous fish. But whether he used a kite to help him is not known, for *he* managed to escape undetected.

The two Oriental rogues were certainly not looking for attention. They would both have been happier had they escaped official notice. But in 1901, a young American girl floated over the streets of Boston on a kite, and she did it solely for the publicity it would bring. Her name was Almenia Rice and she was an aerialist.

Mrs. Rice and her husband Dan needed to advertise the

fact that Almenia was a fearless tightrope walker and trapeze artist. So they built a box kite with wings on the sides, a kite approximately twice Almenia's size. Since the box kite was a new invention—scarcely eight years old—its appearance alone was calculated to draw a crowd. But odder still was Almenia's dress. For though women wearing slacks nowadays is hardly news, in 1901 such things were unheard of. And Almenia Rice was about to perform dressed in men's clothes.

Almenia and Dan tested the box kite by hanging heavy weights from it. It flew steadily in the strong wind. When they were totally pleased with the kite's performance, the Rices took the kite to the roof of 144 Tremont Street in Boston. It was in October and a stiff breeze was blowing.

There, several stories above the street, Almenia stood on the kite frame while her husband held the rope of the kite. She stopped traffic for quite a few minutes as she swayed precariously over the streets. The Boston papers mentioned her and her advertising stunt was a success.

Another publicity seeker was Gilbert Totten Woglom, a toy manufacturer and one of the earliest aerial photographers. He spent years flying kites with cameras and messengers and toys attached to his kite lines. But on May 4, 1895, a Woglom stunt made all the newspapers in New York City, a fact which he duly recorded in his book *Parakites*. On that day, the newly created Washington Arch was to be dedicated in Washington Square in Greenwich Village. A great crowd of people were assembled in the small park and lower Fifth Avenue. Thousands more were in the streets as far up as Seventy-second Street to watch the military show and listen to the oratory of the day. But, as the *New York World* said in its headlines of the planned event, "Woglom's Kites Surpassed It."

What Woglom did was to suspend a ten-foot American flag some 2000 feet above the arch by flying six large kites

When New York's Washington Square was dedicated in 1895,
Gilbert Totten Woglom's display of Old Glory from high-flying
kites stole the headlines from the military parade.

from Judson Memorial Tower, on the south side of the park. The flag, made of bunting, weighed—with its staff—one and five-eighths pounds. The top of the staff was securely fastened directly to the main kite line while the bottom hung loose. The flag rose majestically and stayed there, as one enthusiastic reporter stated in the *New York Press,* "grandly outlined against the Venetian sky that glorified the city's holiday until the celebration was ended."

Another kite enthusiast who captured newspaper headlines for days, and who became the Peter Zenger of kite fliers, was Will Yolen, Western Hemisphere Kite Flying Champion. On October 2, 1965, Yolen was flying kites in Central Park with an eight-foot banner attached that urged the public to vote for John Lindsay for mayor. Suddenly a mounted policeman came by and handed him a summons. What Yolen had done was to violate a city ordinance against distribution of political literature in city parks. Besides, kite flying in New York's Central Park was against the law. There was a statute, remaining on the books from the old horse-and-buggy days of the city, that prohibited kites because they frightened the horses. The horses were almost totally gone from New York. The old law remained.

The American Civil Liberties Union took up Yolen's case on the grounds that his constitutional freedom of speech was being abridged. Five months later, long after Lindsay had won the election, Will Yolen won his case. In a written decision, the Parks' Department law was declared unconstitutional. Kite flying in Central Park was legally open to the public.

Laws against kite flying remain in other places, though. Around airports especially, kite fliers are unwelcome as hazards to navigation. In fact, in 1962, the Federal Aviation Agency in America placed a ban on heavy kites—kites weighing more than five pounds—for a five-mile radius around

As kite flying is not an organized sport, you can see kite fliers almost anywhere. Shown here are children flying modified French military kites on a strip of beach.

airports. It is also illegal to fly kites more than 500 feet from the ground near an airport.

In many lands for centuries kite flying was tabooed for women. In seventeenth-century Japan, when a certain Yui-no Shosetsu tried to overthrow the government and rode on a kite to spy out the palace of Yedo, the court was so taken aback, they forbade the construction of large kites under penalty of death. In France, on October 16, 1736, kite flying was restricted to certain times in public places because of riots which occasionally broke out between rival fliers. In modern America, President Kennedy spoke up for repealing Section 4 of the Act of July 29, 1892, which prohibited flying kites, balloons, or parachutes in the District of Columbia. It was repealed on July 18, 1963.

Now dedicated fliers fly on lonely beaches or in club-sponsored fly-ins such as were organized by the Franklin Kite Club in the 1830s or the equally enthusiastic modern organizations such as the International Kitefliers Association (IKA) and the American Kitefliers Association (AKA). They fly their kites one at a time or in tandem. (The record for the greatest number of kites on a single line belongs to Charles Lohsen of New Jersey. In 1949 he lofted 108 kites on a single string!) According to statistics, nearly forty million kites a year are bought and/or made in America alone. Forty million—and that, of course, does not include the rest of the world on a string.

World
On a
String

Sleep my child, sleep my child,
Where is thy nurse gone?
She is gone to the mountains
To buy thee sweetmeats.
What shall she buy thee?
The thundering drum, the bamboo pipe,
The trundling man, or the paper kite?

—JAPANESE LULLABY

In the Orient the kite was once so familiar to the children
that it made its way into the folk tales, the national holidays,
and even into the gentle lullabies that mothers sang at night.
It was as much a part of the daily rituals as it was a part
of the religious life. Adults and children flew kites with

equal abandon, and it was not any more surprising to see an old Japanese man sitting in a chair, a kitestring in his hand, or a Chinese shopkeeper taking a moment from his duties to fly a kite before his store, than it was to watch the children of these lands making and flying small versions of the colorful toys on the national holidays.

But today many of the festivals have been forgotten the way colorful old costumes have disappeared into musty trunks. They have become memories of the fathers and grandfathers, supplanted by the more "modern" sports of soccer and baseball or other Western borrowings. In fact, the authentic Maori bird-kite is as extinct as the dodo and can only be seen in museums these days.

Adults and children fly kites with equal abandon in Japan as this old print shows.

New Year's Day is a traditional kite-flying time in Japan when the tako *takes to the air in the form of animals, fish, and octagonal warrior kites.*

However, some festivals do still exist, even if the modern world has intruded on the festivities. In Japan, one of those special kite holidays is May 5, Boys' Festival. In Japan it is known as *Tango-no-Sekku*. The aim of the holiday is to encourage the boys to be good, brave, and vigorous. Since in Japan the symbol of vigor is the carp, carp-shaped kites are flown from rooftops or from bamboo poles all day long. These carp kites are hollow paper fish. Wind blows into the open mouths that are fastened onto bamboo hoops and fills the paper bellows. The colorful fish seem to swim in the air. Some of the paper carp kites are over eight feet long. According to legend, the celebration of Boys' Festival began years ago when a boy named Kintaro stood beside a riverbank watching the fishermen at work. Suddenly the boy noticed a man-eating carp swimming toward the unwary workers. Kintaro threw himself into the river and fought and killed the fish. Ever since then, *Tango-no-Sekku* has been celebrated.

Two other large Japanese kite holidays are the Festival of the Cherry Blossom, which is given over to kite fighting, and the New Year's Day kite flying when the *tako* that are flown are in the forms of birds and fans, octopus and tortoises, brightly colored fish, or octagon-shaped warriors.

If a kite is lost in Japan's Sugura province, it is not unusual for search parties to follow the lost toy many miles, or to offer rewards for its recovery.

One of the most unusual kite flights in Japan is an annual event that takes place in Zama, a small village near Tokyo. There a giant 770-square-foot kite is lofted yearly. The kite weighs 581 pounds, more than one fourth of a ton. It requires 200 young men of Zama to hold it steady. The rope used to tether this monster kite is one and a half inches in diameter, and its end is fastened to a long pine log which is weighted down by fifty bags of rice, each weighing 147 pounds.

The Zama kite is square, with a bamboo frame that is lashed together. The bamboo of the main frame is so wide, a man cannot encircle it with his hands. The frame is covered with twenty squares of paper, a paper that is as tough as cloth. Each of the ten-foot-square pieces of paper is laboriously tied to the bamboo framework just before the kite is sent up. This is known as "dressing the kite." Then three to five tails, each 263 feet long, are attached to the kite, the number depending upon the wind's velocity. The giant kite of Zama has at least two dresses—one for ordinary flights and one for extra-special occasions.

When it is time for the flight, the kite is carried to the flying field, a plateau between two mountain ranges. There it is carefully dressed and then laid flat on the ground. After the tails and cords have been adjusted, the monster is sent

In Zama, a village near Tokyo, a giant 770-square-foot kite is sent aloft yearly by a team of sturdy young men who sail the monstrous kite from a plateau between two mountain ranges.

The dragon kite, the most famous kite of China, is made of bamboo disks covered with paper and connected by cords.

up into the air. As it goes up, the ropemen nearest the kite are sometimes pulled off their feet. It is literally a giant tug-of-war with a demon of the sky. No wonder the Zama villagers have been known, since medieval days, as great kite fliers.

The Chinese have a giant kite, too, but it is quite a different kind of monster. It is the famous dragon kite. The dragon kite is a series of light disks made of bamboo covered with paper and connected by cords to keep them equidistant. A sprig of grass is attached to each disk to help the dragon keep its balance. The head disk has a grotesque face drawn upon it and the last disk has a tail. In the wind, the dragon kite seems to wriggle like a giant serpent.

And just as the Japanese have a fish that swims from a pole top, so too the Chinese fly a fish kite. The Chinese fish is flown whenever a boy is born into a family. There is a Chinese saying to the effect that a child, like a fish, should make its own way upstream. If a family has more than one son, the flagpole in front of their house will carry fish of different sizes, each one symbolizing one boy.

One of the popular Chinese holidays when kites take to the air is the Festival of the Lantern Kites on the fifteenth day of January at the Hour of the Ox—midnight. The kites are flown with small candle lanterns attached. And musical kites, too, are very popular still in China.

There are some Koreans who criticize the Chinese, saying that although they know how to *make* beautiful kites, they do not know how to *fly* them. These same critics point out that when a Chinese flier is tired, he will tie his kite-string to a tree and lie down and watch it.

Kite flying reached Korea from the other Oriental countries in the first century A.D. But once there, the kite design—a rectangle—altered little, even to the present day. On the other hand, the Chinese and Japanese kites underwent marvelous changes and it is these latter kites that are world famous for ornamentation and design.

Perhaps the Korean kite critics are merely expressing an extension of the political rivalries that have long existed between Korea and China. Or perhaps it is because Koreans take their kite flying so seriously that they have a National Kite Day. On this day, the mothers write on the wings of the kites a list of toys and playthings which their children would like to receive. Then the kites are loosed to carry these wishes away where, hopefully, the gods will read them. Also, on the fourteenth day of January, a Korean mother writes her son's name and birthdate on the bamboo frame of a kite plus a wish that the year's misfortunes be carried away. Then a piece of sulphur paper is attached to the kitestring and set afire. When the sulphur burns through, it also burns the string and the kite flies away, bearing the boy's bad luck with it.

In Thailand, the country of the great kite fights, kiting begins in March when the monsoon from the east starts to blow. Kite dealers roam the streets hawking their wares. And children fly kites less for pleasure than as preparation for the more sophisticated sport of kite fighting. They are, in a sense, training for the big leagues. But as popular as kite fighting is in Thailand, it is not the only kind of kiting. On the Royal Cremation Ground is held an annual festival which is attended by the king and the royal family. Besides the kite fights, there are contests for the most beautiful and most original kites.

There is also an old Thai legend called *Suvarnahansa* in which a lover is led to his lady by following the strings of a runaway kite. And once, in ancient Thailand, when it was still called Siam, kites were flown to call up the seasonal winds.

Kite fighting is popular, too, in Tibet. In the autumn, when the rains are over, the bazaars suddenly sprout with bright-colored kites. Both adults and children buy these paper toys and fly them from the rooftops.

In India, where kites were introduced either by the Malayan or Chinese immigrants, kite fighting is the most popular kind of kite activity. And kite making is a dignified profession. But there is a gentler side to Indian kite flying, too. Not long ago, the Maharajah of Bharatpur took his second wife on a kite flying honeymoon. This same maharajah has a "kite bearer" who does the actual lofting of the kite. Once the kite is in the sky, he hands the string to his master.

In the Islamic world, the earliest reference to kites was in the ninth century. In *The Book of Animals*, Abu Uthman al-Jahiz described kites "made of Chinese carton and paper."

Greek kite flying, though not confined to a single day, is most popular on Clean Monday, the day that signals the end of carnival and the beginning of Lent. On that day kites pepper the skies all over the Greek countryside, but are especially concentrated on Philapapos Hill, across from the Acropolis.

In Polynesia, where kite flying was once associated with the old religions, kites are no longer the popular sport of kings and warriors. Where once the kite was honored and revered as a god, and where old men had flying parties

The Maharajah of Bharatpur (right), who took his wife on a kite-flying honeymoon, entertains champion flier Will Yolen with an exhibition of Indian kites in front of his hunting palace.

On Clean Monday, Greek children take their kites to Philapapos Hill and there, across from the Acropolis, they fly them as a sign that Lent has begun.

at which a point of honor was that the kite be lost to view in the clouds and the ancients sometimes slept out on the mountainsides after tying their kitestrings securely to the trees, kite flying has been slowly losing its popularity. Only occasionally are kites seen in the islands now.

In some Maori tribes there were special huts or sheds

built for large kites. There the kites were placed on racks or platforms and the evening before a scheduled flight they would be removed and placed outside where the dew could fall on them. This was so the moisture would toughen the leaf covering of the kite, making it less liable to injury.

Maori kites were often hawk-shaped with outspread wings and measured as much as ten to twelve feet from wingtip to wingtip. They were made of leaves sewn onto tea-tree twigs that were stained alternately red and black. The body of the bird was topped by a manlike head made of linen or calico and decorated with shaved hawk feathers. A fine model of such a kite is in the Auckland Museum.

In the olden days, these large kites were maneuvered by thirty-man teams. Often live birds were set loose inside

In Polynesia, where kite flying was once the sport of kings and gods, only a few simple kites are raised over the beaches today.

the kite's head and they made a rattling and grumbling in the wind. But this was no sport for children. The bird kite had horns made of plucked albatross plumes and if the kite took a sudden dive, it was extremely dangerous. More than one man was reported to have been killed, his body pierced by the horns of the falling kite.

In the European countries and in America, kite flying is now undergoing a revival. Springtime and summer in these countries are considered kite-flying weather. Rather than nationally sponsored kite holidays, special kite contests are usually under the sponsorship of a single city or civic

A man-sized version of the ancient Maori hawk-kite. In the old days these kites were ten to twelve feet from tip to tip with two dangerous horns projecting from the head.

In the East, special holidays are set aside for kite flying, but in the West any day that is filled with light breezes and a golden sun is the time to fly a kite.

organization. It is not unusual to see colorful kites fluttering over crowded beaches or swinging between mountains on weekends and vacations.

Why are there no Western kite holidays? In the Eastern countries kite flying was a part of religious ceremony and so there kites are still associated with traditional holiday activities. In the West, kite flying developed in a more secular path, though it branched wildly from kite skiing to scientific kiting, from a Central Park kite-in for peace to a university sponsored kite-designing contest.

There are no set holy days or holidays for flying in the West. Only good flying days and bad. When the sun shimmers like a gold coin in the sky, and the wind whispers longingly in the trees, when breezes catch and pull at leaves and toss the clouds across the sky—these are the times for kite flying in the West.

Kites Today— An Epilogue

Ask someone to describe a kite and he will usually reply, "A toy made of sticks and paper." Ask someone to draw a kite, and he will almost invariably make a diamond-shaped object with a long tail at one end and a string that hangs to the ground. But a stick-and-paper, diamond-shaped kite is not the only kind of kite available, even if it is probably the best known. And even though it is extremely popular, this kind of kite is no longer typical of kites today. For example, nylon cloth has replaced paper for the kite covering in many instances, and kites are also constructed of sail cloth, silk, or even of a tough plastic film. Then, too, the strings of kites are made of various materials, from ordinary wrapping twine to the finest kind of nylon line. Even piano wire has been used—with the large meteoro-

The diamond-shaped flat kite is the best-known kite in the West. Here sailors on the U. S. S. Frontier *send up a simple kite over the Pacific Ocean.*

logical kites. Kites come with big tails, with small tails, and with no tails at all. The variations seem almost endless.

Kite flying can be one of the world's least expensive sports. There are two-stick paper kites that can be purchased for as little as ten cents in candy stores, dime stores, and novelty shops. But kite flying can also be a sport for the rich. A fully equipped Indian-made fighter kite with its cutting string begins at five dollars and goes up and up in price, according to size, design, weight of string. French military kites start at about six dollars and will go as high as your kite budget and string will allow.

The most popular kites today can be found in both expensive and inexpensive models. They may be purchased at local stores or ordered from specialty houses such as New York's Go Fly A Kite Store; or they may be made at home with instructions found in hobby books and magazines.

According to the International Kitefliers Association, the following are the five basic kinds of kites, of which the first three are the most popular in the West:

The bow or Eddy kite looks like the flat kite but has a curved center stick. John Aymar, who has done a lot of work with the bow kites, flew kites with the late William Eddy.

Flat Kite—a kite made with crossed sticks and a flat surface. The simplest flat kite is the two-stick or Diamond Kite, and it is found in any store that sells kites. There are also three-stick and four-stick varieties, with octagonal or hexagonal coverings. A tail is a necessary part of the Flat Kite.

Bow Kite—also known as the Malay or Eddy Kite. It is essentially a diamond shape with the front bowed instead of flat. It needs no tail and is one of the most stable kinds of kite in the world.

Box Kite—developed by Hargrave, is a rectangular kite. It is the kite that was used in many meteorological experiments and is considered an "angled" rather than a flat kite. There are many variations of the box kite built by the early scientific kite experimenters. One of the popular variations is the French Military Kite, which was used by the French for army observations. It is a box kite with wings.

130

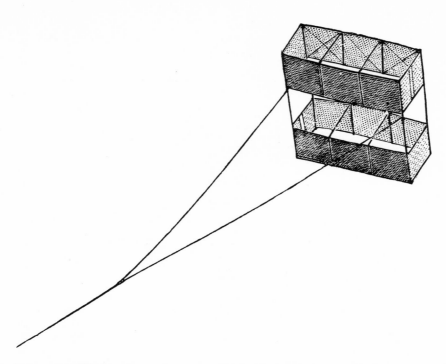

Lawrence Hargrave made a number of cellular kites before coming up with the now famous box which was the favorite of meteorologists for many years.

Non-rigid Kite—first created by Francis M. Rogallo and called by him the Flexikite. The non-rigid kite's shape is dictated by shroud lines. These kites and their variants—such as kite parachutes, kite balloons, and the Puerto Rican *chiringa*—are only beginning to come into popularity. The non-rigid kite is, to all intents and purposes, indestructible since it can crash to the ground or fall into the water and not break.

Novelty Kite—includes many shapes and sizes. The bulk of Oriental kites fall into this category for the Western flier. The Indian fighter kite, the Thai Owl Kite, the Chinese Butterfly Kite, the Dragon Kite, the fish (carp) kites and other exotic toys that are known by some of the more sophisticated kite fliers are considered Novelty Kites. They are often a mixture of several other kinds of kites. They are the most difficult to find and the most complicated to build.

Will Yolen and friends prepare to loft a tremendous French military kite from a beach.

Today a sixth kind of kite might be added to the IKA list. It is the *objet d'art*, the kite as a piece of sculpture. Though kites-as-parachutes were an idea that the world-famous artist Leonardo da Vinci toyed with in the Renaissance, it was not until late in our own century that serious artists began to create kites simply as art—with no thought at all to flying them.

In the forefront of this artistic venture is Japanese painter

The flexible kite invented by Francis M. Rogallo not only has proven invaluable to air and space science, but also has given rise to many variations such as this flexible bird-kite.

Novelty kites are popular in the East, especially in Japan where miniature bird and insect kites dot the skies with their colorful wings.

and sculptor Fumio Yoshimura. His sculptured kites, begun in 1963, have been exhibited in museums and private collections around the world. They range in size from tiny "bug" kites a few inches wide to large designs some eighteen feet across. And many art, architecture, and design schools throughout the United States assign kite-making projects to their students in the spring. The object is to be aesthetically—if not aerodynamically—sound.

In the United States there are two national kite clubs. The International Kitefliers Association is a loose-knit organization headed by Western Hemisphere Kite Flying Cham-

Sculptor Fumio Yoshimura's kites-as-art have been exhibited throughout the world and give further proof of the ever-evolving world on a string.

pion, Will Yolen. Its avowed purpose—"world-wide friends through kite flying"—is attained through exchange of letters and visits and by goodwill trips made by the president. Each member carries a membership card. There are no dues.

The American Kitefliers Association is a kite club exclusively for fliers over twenty-one years of age. For the club membership fee of five dollars annually, a quarterly publication called *Kite Tales* is received. It is a large mimeographed compilation of kite stories, pictures, facts, instructions for making and flying kites, and assorted bits of history lovingly put together by the club president, Robert Ingraham, a

New Mexico businessman. Except for the IKA and the AKA, kite clubs and activities are locally sponsored. Often a city or town will hold kite tournaments under the auspices of the Police Athletic League, the Boy Scouts, the PTA, or similar organizations. These tournaments are of two kinds. Either there is a kite *flying* contest in which height and maneuvering are judged or there is a judging of home-made kites for beauty, originality, and similar qualities.

The only way to discover if the kite is *your* contract of glory is to make or buy a kite of your own. Then you must find a spot where the wind is right. Now take out your wind-bird, your sky dragon, your serpent of the air and send it as high and as far as you dare. Perhaps then you will begin to discover what the poet e. e. cummings meant when he wrote that the end of a string is a wonderful thing.

Indeed, it is a whole world—a world on a string.

The only way to discover if the kite is your "contract of glory" is to make or buy a kite of your own and fly it.

Books
For Further
Reading

Best, Eldon, *Games & Pastimes of Children*. Dominion Museum Bulletin Number 8. Wellington, N.Z., 1925.

Broomfield, G. A., *Pioneer of the Air, The Life and Times of Col. S. F. Cody*. Aldershot, England: Gale & Polden, Ltd., 1953.

Chadwick, Nora K., *"The Kite: A Study in Polynesian Tradition." Journal of the Royal Anthropological Institute of Great Britain and Ireland*, Vol. LXI (1931), pp. 455–91.

Fisher, Sydney George, *The True Benjamin Franklin*. Philadelphia: J. B. Lippincott, 1900.

Fraser, Antonia, *A History of Toys*. New York: Delacorte Press, 1966.

Gibbs-Smith, C. H., *A History of Flying*. London: B. T. Batsford, Ltd., 1953.

————, *The Invention of the Aeroplane*. London: Faber & Faber, 1966.

Gordon, Lesley, *Peepshow Into Paradise, A History of Children's Toys*. London: George C. Harrap & Co., Ltd., 1953.

Hart, Clive, *Kites, An Historical Survey*. New York: Frederick Praeger, 1967.

Hodgson, J. E., *The History of Aeronautics in Great Britain*. London: Oxford University Press, 1924.

Jackson, Mrs. F. Nevill, *Toys of Other Days*. New York: Charles Scribner's Sons, 1908.

Jue, David F., *Chinese Kites*. Rutland, Vermont: Charles E. Tuttle Co., 1967.

Kettlekemp, Larry, *Kites*. New York: William Morrow & Company, 1959.

Laufer, Berthold, *The Prehistory of Aviation*. Field Museum of Natural History Anthropological Series, Vol. XVIII, No. 1. Chicago, 1928.

Lee, Arthur Gould, *The Flying Cathedral*. London: Methuen & Co., Ltd., 1965.

Luce, W. B., *Kites and Experiments in Aerial Photography*. Hingham Centre, Mass., 1898.

Neal, Harry Edward, *The Story of the Kite*. New York: The Vanguard Press, Inc., 1954.

Needham, Joseph, *Science and Civilization in China*. Vol. 4, Part 2. Cambridge: Cambridge University Press, 1965.

Rotch, A. Lawrence, *Sounding the Ocean of Air*. London: Society For Promoting Christian Knowledge, 1900.

Sakamoto, Kazuya, *Japanese Toys: Playing With History*. Rutland, Vermont: Charles E. Tuttle Co., 1965.

Taylor, John W. R. *A Picture History of Flight*. London: Edward Hulton, 1959.

Voisin, Gabriel, *Men, Women, and 10,000 Kites*. London: Putnam & Co., Ltd., 1963.

Woglom, Gilbert Totten, *Parakites*. New York: G. P. Putnam's Sons, 1896.

Yolen, Will, *A Young Sportsman's Guide to Kite Flying*. Camden, New Jersey: Thomas Nelson & Sons, 1963.

Index

Photo
Acknowledgements

The author and The World Publishing Company wish to thank the following
for permission to reproduce the illustrations in this book:

Bernice P. Bishop Museum	64, 65, 125, 126
George H. Cardozo	132
Chinese Government Information Service	120
Colorado State University	33
Environmental Science Services Administration	29, 40, 41
Field Musuem of Natural History	16
Go Fly A Kite Store	88, 134
Japanese National Tourist Organization	92, 93, 117, 119
Tom Lesley	2–3
London Illustrated News	80
National Aeronautics and Space Administration	56, 57, 59, 133
National Geographic Society	51, 52
North American Aviation	58
Science Museum, London	47
Scientific American	54, 55, 101
The Smithsonian Institution	20, 22, 102
Special Devices Division, Bureau of Aeronautics	83
David Stemple	94, 95, 127
U.S. Army	40, 82
U.S. Navy	43, 129
U.S. Department of Commerce, Weather Bureau	30
Don Wellenkamp	84

ABOUT THE AUTHOR

JANE YOLEN is the author of *The Minstrel and the Mountain* and the Caldecott runner-up *The Emperor and the Kite*, and *Greyling*. Formerly a children's book editor, she now devotes full time to writing. She lives with her husband, a photographer and teacher, and their two children in Conway, Mass.

1   2   3   4   5   72   71   70   69   68